Llyfrgell Sir POWYS County Library
Llandrindod Wells LD1 5LD

www.powys.gov.uk/libraries

Llyfrgell Machynlleth
Machynlleth Library
Ffôn/Tel: 01654 702322

17 JAI
-3 JAI

2 0 NOV 2012

Llyfrgell y Trallw
Library

D0830901

Powys

37218 00484623 9

Rose Elliot
Classic Vegetarian Recipes

Rose Elliot
Classic Vegetarian Recipes
75 signature dishes

hamlyn

To all my family and friends, with love

An Hachette UK Company
www.hachette.co.uk

First published in Great Britain in 2011 by Hamlyn,
a division of Octopus Publishing Group Ltd
Endeavour House, 189 Shaftesbury Avenue
London WC2H 8JY

www.octopusbooks.co.uk

Copyright © Octopus Publishing Group Ltd 2011
Text copyright © Rose Elliot 2011

This book includes a selection of new and previously published recipes.
Recipes that have been published before are taken from the following Rose
Elliot titles: *Vegetarian Supercook*, *Veggie Chic*, *The Supreme Vegetarian Cookbook*,
Vegetarian Dishes of the World, *Vegetarian Four Seasons*, *The New Vegetarian
Cookbook*, *The Classic Vegetarian Cookbook*, *Vegetarian Barbecues and Grills*.

All rights reserved. No part of this work may be reproduced or utilized
in any form or by any means, electronic or mechanical, including
photocopying, recording or by any information storage and retrieval
system, without the prior written permission of the publisher.

Rose Elliot asserts the moral right to be identified as the author
of this work.

ISBN 978-0-600-62179-9

A CIP catalogue record for this book is available from the British Library

Printed and bound in China

10 9 8 7 6 5 4 3 2 1

Both metric and imperial measurements are given for the recipes.
Use one set of measures only, not a mixture of both.

Ovens should be preheated to the specified temperature. If using a
fan-assisted oven, follow the manufacturer's instructions for adjusting
the time and temperature. Grills should also be preheated.

This book includes dishes made with nuts and nut derivatives.
It is advisable for those with known allergic reactions to nuts and nut
derivatives and those who may be potentially vulnerable to these
allergies, such as pregnant and nursing mothers, invalids, the elderly,
babies and children, to avoid dishes made with nuts and nut oils.
It is also prudent to check the labels of preprepared ingredients for
the possible inclusion of nut derivatives.

The Department of Health advises that eggs should not be consumed
raw. This book contains some dishes made with raw or lightly cooked
eggs. It is prudent for more vulnerable people such as pregnant and
nursing mothers, invalids, the elderly, babies and young children to
avoid uncooked or lightly cooked dishes made with eggs.

Contents

Introduction

Vegetarian cookery has come of age. From simple beginnings with Pythagoras in the West and Confucius and the Buddha in the East, through the austerity of the food reform movement in the late nineteenth century, and the brown rice and hippies of the 1960s and 1970s, it has grown and blossomed into the glorious, vibrant, colourful, eclectic cuisine that it is today, and it's continuing to evolve all the time.

What I love about the cuisine is that because the only criterion is that no meat or fish, or products made from them (such as gelatine, rennet or stock), are used you can be as inventive and outrageous as you like! Vegetarian cookery encourages you to be creative, and try new and exciting combinations of ingredients, flavours and textures.

In addition, because the cuisine has an ideological rather than a geographical base, it embraces dishes from all over the world that meet the vegetarian criterion. So we have spicy curries from India rubbing shoulders with creamy hummus from the Middle East, wild mushroom tempura from the Far East, and bubble-and-squeak cakes with beetroot relish from the UK. It's stimulating and empowering to have so many mouth-watering possibilities. Far from being limiting, vegetarian cookery is expansive, freeing and inspiring.

So, how to choose the 80 classic recipes for this collection? For me, as well being full of flavour and looking good, a classic vegetarian recipe has a simplicity and practicality about it and is straightforward and undemanding to make. Most of all, it's something that people really like making and eating. So I chose the recipes people always mention, the ones they tell me they love, the ones they always ask for, the ones my family relish and want me to cook time and time again.

I hope you too will enjoy them, and that they will become staples of your own repertoire and the basis of many tasty, happy meals.

All the recipes are straightforward, and some are very quick and easy. An excellent way to bring more variety to your cooking is to make a note of recipes that appeal and plan on making one or two new ones every week. Read the recipes through,

7

INTRODUCTION

make a note of the ingredients, and any baking tins or utensils you need, and add them to your shopping list. You'll soon build up an exciting store cupboard and a range of equipment to make cooking easier and more fun while enjoying some wonderful meals. Here are some notes to guide you. Have fun!

Kitchen equipment

You don't need lots of fancy things for vegetarian cookery: a decent chopping board, a good knife and something to sharpen it with, and a box grater are the essentials. I also like a small knife with a sharp, serrated blade for slicing delicate things like tomatoes and peaches, and a fine microplane grater for grating ginger and even garlic. An electric hand blender is very useful for puréeing in the pan, and I wouldn't be without my food processor: it saves so much time. Other electrical appliances that I find really useful are a lemon squeezer that remains on my work surface, ready for instant action (so useful and time-saving if you like fresh lemon or lime juice as a flavouring), a coffee grinder that I use just for spices and seeds, and a whisk.

Ingredients

There are so many delicious and exciting ingredients from all over the world that can be used in vegetarian cookery. Here are some of the most important ones.

Fresh vegetables and fruits

These are the basis of vegetarian cookery: sparkling fresh vegetables of all kinds and luscious fruits. I'm sure that's one of the main reasons why statistics always show this way of eating to be so health-giving: getting your 'five a day' (or even ten, or fifteen!) happens almost without trying. Keep vegetables and fruits in the fridge if appropriate.

Milk, cheese and eggs

I only ever use soya milk, rather than dairy, and cheese is always vegetarian – that is, made with vegetarian rennet. There are vegetarian versions of most cheeses. Traditional Parmesan cheese is not vegetarian but you can buy Parmesan-style Italian hard cheeses that are (one large supermarket has one in its basic foods range). Vegetarian Gruyère is available, but you might need to go online to track it down – or use Emmental or even Edam as a substitute. I find the staff at cheese counters helpful when I want to find a vegetarian alternative for a particular cheese. Some very light soft cheeses may contain gelatine (made from, amongst other things, the bones and hoofs of animals), as do some yogurts, so read the labels carefully. Eggs are always organic free-range – medium or large, it doesn't really matter for most recipes.

Veganizing recipes: Vegans don't eat eggs or dairy produce and many don't eat honey (though some do). Some recipes in this book are in fact naturally vegan and others can easily be made suitable for vegans by using pure vegetable spread instead of butter, and soya milk, cream and cream cheese, all of which are widely available. When applicable, use pastry made with pure vegetable fat. Vegan cheeses, made without milk, are available from health shops and can sometimes be used instead of dairy cheese, but many of them do not melt in the same way, so you can't always make a direct swap when a recipe calls for the cheese to be cooked.

Cereals and grains

I use Basmati rice, brown or white or both; I also like a mix of Basmati and wild rice that you can buy in supermarkets, and carnaroli for risotto. Quinoa (pronounced keen-wa) is an interesting and nutritious grain and can be bought in health shops and supermarkets.

Nuts and seeds

Buy in small quantities and keep in the fridge or freezer if possible. Pecans, almonds, pine nuts, walnuts and cashews are useful. Salted macadamia nuts and salted peanuts are good stand-bys, especially for garnishes, as are sesame seeds.

Beans and lentils

Dried beans and lentils are lovely and not much trouble to prepare once you get into the habit: soak them overnight, then boil hard for 10 minutes and follow with a slow simmer until they're done. It does save time to use canned ones, though, and I've used them throughout this book except in the lentil soup, and in the falafel recipe where dried chickpeas are needed. Frozen podded edamame beans, which look a bit like broad beans that have been popped out of their grey skins, are full of protein and the opened pack can be kept in the freezer.

Herbs and spices

I always have some pots of fresh herbs on my kitchen window sill; I love the look of them, and they're handy when I want a small quantity or a garnish. If a recipe needs a serious amount of fresh herbs, it's best to buy a bag of them specially for the purpose and keep it in the fridge. Some of the more robust herbs – bay, thyme, marjoram, rosemary and sage – are as good dried as fresh, if not better, unless you want to use the leaves for a garnish.

It's best to buy dried herbs and spices in small quantities so that they're fresh when you need them. Chilli powder and/or crushed red chilli flakes, ground coriander, ground cumin and turmeric are all useful; I also love cardamom, star anise and nutmeg – which is most flavourful if you buy it whole and grate it fresh when you need it. A nutmeg grater with a compartment to keep the nutmegs makes this quick and easy.

Store-cupboard basics

A well-stocked store cupboard makes all the difference to the ease and joy of cooking and is something that you can build up gradually. These are some favourites that are used in the recipes in this book.

Alcohol: Make sure it's veggie; this means fino sherry and crusted port.

Cans, packets and jars: Beans and lentils, see opposite. A packet or two of tofu in the fridge (or the UHT type, which is also good and keeps well without chilling). A jar or two of chargrilled artichoke hearts for adding to salads, rice dishes or for making a quick frittata. Some olives – I like Kalamata ones in a jar – and capers; I especially like caper berries for salads and garnishes. Canned chopped tomatoes in juice, increasingly to be found in cartons; it's always worth buying good-quality ones.

Coconut milk; I prefer to buy the normal milk and reduce the fat if I want to by adding some water. I also keep jars of good-quality mayonnaise, Dijon mustard and horseradish sauce in my fridge.

Flours: Plain and self-raising; wholemeal, especially spelt. A small bag of chickpea flour, sometimes called gram flour, for making bhajis. Cornflour; I like to mix this with water to make a paste for coating spicy cakes before dipping them in dried breadcrumbs and then frying them.

Oils: Extra virgin olive oil for dressings, and a lighter one for shallow-frying; rapeseed for deep-frying. A small bottle of grapeseed oil is useful if you want to brush something with a tasteless oil. Toasted sesame oil for Asian dishes – it imparts an immediately Asian flavour.

Pastry: I love to make my own shortcrust pastry, but I buy filo and puff. Look for an all-butter puff pastry, or pastry made with pure vegetable fat if you want a vegan one.

Flavourings

Garlic. Ginger; keep some in the fridge ready to grate whenever required. Fresh limes and lemons. Soy sauce; a nice natural one like shoyu or tamari, made without caramel, colourings and so on. Vegetable bouillon powder for making vegetable stock. Vinegars: rice, cider, red wine, balsamic, raspberry. Black pepper in a pepper mill. Vanilla; nothing beats the flavour of the pods, and real vanilla extract in a bottle is also useful. Salt: sea salt, the kind you can crush in your fingers is fine – my favourite by far, though, is the coarse grey sea salt from Guérande (*gros sel de Guérande*). You can buy it at any large supermarket in France and I stock up when I'm there. When I get home, I spread it out on a baking sheet and dry it in a cool oven, then grind it to a powder in the food processor, ready for use without the faff of having to use a grinder at the table.

Sweetenings: Fair Trade caster sugar. Maple syrup. Honey. Condensed milk: normal for making ice cream and caramelized for banoffi pie.

Soups, Starters and Snacks

Red Lentil and Roasted Pepper Soup

SERVES 6

2 red onions, cut into
2.5 cm (1 inch) pieces

2 teaspoons olive oil

2 red peppers, halved,
cored and deseeded

4 garlic cloves, unpeeled

small handful of thyme

125 g (4 oz) split red
lentils

600 ml (1 pint) water

2 bay leaves

salt and pepper

chopped basil and
a few shavings of
Parmesan-style
cheese, to serve

*I love this soup! It's so easy to make, yet tastes and looks really special,
glowing with the vibrant colour of the lentils and peppers.*

1 Toss the onions in the olive oil and put them on a
baking sheet, along with the peppers, which don't need
oiling. Roast in a preheated oven, 180°C (350°F), Gas Mark
4, for 30 minutes, or until the vegetables are nearly tender,
then add the garlic and thyme to the baking sheet and
cook for 10 minutes more, until all the vegetables are
tender. Set aside to cool.

2 Meanwhile, wash the red lentils and put them into a
saucepan with the water and bay leaves. Bring to the boil,
then simmer for 15 minutes, or until the lentils are soft and
pale coloured. Remove and discard the bay leaves.

3 Rub off as much of the skin from the peppers as you
can – get rid of any very dark bits, but don't worry about
being too particular. Pop the garlic out of its skin with
your fingers. Put the peppers and garlic into a food
processor with the onion (discard the thyme). Add the
lentils together with their cooking liquid and whiz to a
smooth, creamy consistency, thinning it with a little water,
if necessary.

4 Return the mixture to the pan and reheat gently. Season
to taste with salt and pepper, then ladle into warmed bowls
and top each with basil and thin shavings of Parmesan.

Chunky Bean and Vegetable Soup

Simple, classic, delicious and full of goodness. It's also delicious made with a bit less liquid and served with baked potatoes.

SERVES 4

1 tablespoon olive oil

2 onions, chopped

250 g (8 oz) carrots,
   cut into 1 cm (½ inch)
   chunks

250 g (8 oz) parsnips,
   cut into 1 cm (½ inch)
   chunks

250 g (8 oz) leeks,
   trimmed, cleaned and
   sliced

250 g (8 oz) cabbage,
   sliced

a few thyme sprigs

2 bay leaves

410 g (13½ oz) can
   cannellini beans,
   drained

1.2 litres (2 pints)
   vegetable stock

salt and pepper

chopped parsley,
   to garnish

wholemeal bread
   and grated cheese,
   to serve (optional)

1 Heat the olive oil in a large saucepan, add the onions, cover and cook for 5 minutes. Then add the carrots, parsnips, leeks, cabbage, thyme sprigs and bay leaves, and stir to lightly coat them all with the oil. Cover the pan and cook gently for a further 10 minutes.

2 Add the beans and vegetable stock, bring to the boil, then cover and leave to simmer over a gentle heat for 30 minutes.

3 Season with salt and pepper, serve in warm bowls and top each with a scattering of chopped parsley. Serve with wholemeal bread and grated cheese, if liked.

Leek and Potato Soup

SERVES 4–6

- 25 g (1 oz) butter or olive oil
- 700 g (1 lb 7 oz) potatoes, peeled and diced
- 3 leeks, trimmed, cleaned and sliced
- 1 litre (1¾ pints) water
- 1 teaspoon vegetable bouillon powder
- 3–4 tablespoons double cream or non-dairy cream (optional)
- salt and pepper
- chopped parsley, to garnish (optional)

For me, this ties with Lentil Soup with Cumin (see opposite) as the most all-healing, all-comforting soup: the 'chicken soup' of vegetarian cuisine, if you like.

1 Heat the butter or olive oil in a large saucepan, then add the potatoes and leeks. Cover and cook gently for 15–20 minutes, stirring often to prevent the vegetables sticking – this slow cooking of the leeks and potatoes is the secret to making this soup taste really good.

2 Add the water and vegetable bouillon powder, stir, then simmer for 5–10 minutes, until the potatoes and leeks are tender.

3 You can purée this or leave it chunky, depending on your preference, then add the cream, if using.

4 Season with salt and pepper, and serve in warm bowls, sprinkled with a little chopped parsley, if liked.

Lentil Soup with Cumin

SERVES 4

225 g (7½ oz) split red lentils

1.2 litres (2 pints) vegetable stock or water

1 large onion, chopped

2 garlic cloves, crushed

1 teaspoon ground cumin

salt and pepper

A classic, nourishing, warming soup that can also double as dhal to serve with curry or over steamed vegetables, depending on how much stock or water you add.

1 Wash the lentils, then put them into a large saucepan with the vegetable stock or water, onion, garlic and cumin. Bring to the boil and simmer gently for 15–20 minutes, until the lentils are cooked.

2 Purée the lentils and liquid in a liquidizer or food processsor, or rub through a sieve.

3 Season with salt and pepper and reheat the soup gently. Serve in warm bowls. This makes a thickish soup but you can, of course, thin it down with more stock or water.

Tomato Soup with Basil

SERVES 4

15 g (½ oz) butter or olive oil

1 onion, chopped

350 g (11½ oz) potatoes, peeled and diced

450 g (14½ oz) tomatoes, skinned and sliced, or 400 g (13 oz) can tomatoes

900 ml (1½ pints) water

1 teaspoon vegetable bouillon powder

salt and pepper

basil leaves, to garnish

So simple, yet so good, especially when made with luscious summer tomatoes. The version with canned tomatoes is also lovely and makes me think of warm sunny days, even in midwinter!

1 Heat the butter or olive oil in a large saucepan, then add the onion. Cover and cook gently for 5 minutes, so that the onion softens without browning.

2 Add the potatoes, cover again, and cook gently for a further 5–10 minutes, then add the tomatoes and cook for 4–5 minutes. Stir from time to time and do not allow the vegetables to brown.

3 Add the water and bouillon powder, cover the pan and simmer for 15–20 minutes, until the potatoes are tender.

4 Liquidize or blend the soup, then, for perfection, pour it through a sieve back into the pan. Reheat gently and season with salt and pepper if needed.

5 Serve in warm bowls, garnished with basil leaves.

SOUPS, STARTERS AND SNACKS

Twice-baked Individual Soufflés

SERVES 8 AS
A STARTER OR
4 AS A MAIN
COURSE

butter, for greasing

8 tablespoons grated Parmesan-style cheese

225 g (7½ oz) curd or skim-milk cheese

4 egg yolks and 5 egg whites

150 g (5 oz) Gruyère cheese, grated

salt and pepper

I always use smooth white cheese as a base for my soufflés instead of a thick sauce. It's easier, and the results are light and delicious. These freeze well too.

1 Generously grease 8 ramekins, dariole moulds or cups, then sprinkle ½ tablespoon of the Parmesan-style cheese inside each one.

2 Put the curd or skim-milk cheese into a bowl and mash it until it's smooth, then gradually mix in the egg yolks and half the Gruyère. Season well with salt and pepper.

3 Whisk the egg whites with a clean, greasefree whisk until they are standing in peaks, and stir a heaped tablespoonful into the egg yolk mixture to loosen it. Gently fold in the remaining egg whites. Season with salt and pepper.

4 Spoon the mixture into the ramekins, moulds or cups: it can come level with their tops, but don't pile it up any higher. Stand them in a roasting tin, pour in enough boiling water to come halfway up the sides and bake in a preheated oven, 180°C (350°F), Gas Mark 4, for 15 minutes, until the soufflés are risen and set. Remove them from the oven and leave them to get cold – they'll sink a bit.

5 Loosen their edges and turn them out (it's easiest to turn them out on to your hand), then transfer them to an ovenproof serving dish. Sprinkle each soufflé with some of the remaining Gruyère, then with the rest of the Parmesan-style cheese. They can now wait until you are ready to bake them.

6 Preheat the oven to 220°C (425°F), Gas Mark 7, and bake the soufflés for 15–20 minutes, or until they are puffed up and golden brown. Serve at once.

Stilton Pâté with Roasted Beetroots

SERVES 4

200 g (7 oz) low-fat soft cream cheese

1 teaspoon Dijon mustard

200 g (7 oz) Stilton cheese, roughly crumbled

1 tablespoon vegetarian port or fino sherry

pepper

dill sprigs, to garnish

rustic bread, to serve

ROASTED BEETROOTS

450 g (14½ oz) baby beetroots, preferably no bigger than plums

olive oil, for rubbing

CHICORY SALAD

2–3 heads of chicory

1 bunch of watercress

50 g (2 oz) walnuts

I love this combination of sweet, dense beetroot and silky, tangy Stilton dip served with crisp chicory, peppery watercress and a crunch of walnuts.

1 If the beetroots still have leaves attached, cut these off about 5 cm (2 inches) from the beetroot. Scrub the beetroots gently, being careful not to pierce the skin, and leave the long 'tail' on, if still attached. Rub the beetroots with a little olive oil, wrap them lightly in a piece of foil and bake in a preheated oven, 200°C (400°F), Gas Mark 6, for 1–1½ hours, or until tender right through when pierced with a knife. You could uncover them for the last 30 minutes or so, but you don't want them to get too crisp. I like to eat them skins and all, but most people rub off the skins before eating.

2 While the beetroots are cooking, prepare the pâté. Whiz the cream cheese, mustard, Stilton and port or sherry to a cream in a food processor. Season with a little pepper.

3 Mix the ingredients for the salad together.

4 To serve, put a spoonful of the Stilton pâté on each plate (or spread on a slice of bread, if you like) with some of the beetroot – baby ones can be left whole, larger ones cut as necessary – and one or two feathery sprigs of dill. Coarsely grind some pepper over the top and serve with the salad and rustic bread.

Avocado with Raspberry Vinaigrette

SERVES 4
2 ripe avocados

RASPBERRY
VINAIGRETTE

350 g (11½ oz) fresh
  raspberries, washed,
  or frozen raspberries,
  thawed

6 teaspoons water

6 teaspoons caster
  sugar

2 tablespoons
  raspberry or wine
  vinegar

4 tablespoons olive oil

salt and pepper

TO GARNISH

thyme sprigs

a few pink peppercorns
  (optional)

Make the raspberry vinaigrette in advance so that you can assemble this dish in minutes. I like to have it on the table ready to greet my guests when they sit down.

1 First make a raspberry coulis. Blend the raspberries with the water and sugar in a liquidizer or food processor. Sieve and turn into a saucepan. Bring to the boil and boil for 1 minute to make the coulis clear and glossy. Cool and refrigerate until needed.

2 Make the vinaigrette by mixing the raspberry coulis, vinegar and oil. Season with salt and pepper.

3 Halve the avocados and carefully remove the skin and stones. Place half an avocado cut-side down on a palette knife, then use another knife to cut it across into fairly thin slices.

4 Drizzle the vinaigrette on to the centre of each of 4 individual serving plates.

5 Carefully slide the sliced avocado off the palette knife and on to the raspberry vinaigrette, so that the avocado half keeps its shape.

6 Repeat the process with the remaining avocado halves. Garnish with thyme sprigs, and a scattering of pink peppercorns, if liked. Serve immediately.

Bruschette with Three Toppings

MAKES 24

1 baguette or
  rosemary loaf

dried rosemary
  (if using a plain
  baguette)

olive oil

salt and pepper

**AUBERGINE
CAVIAR**

2 aubergines

1–2 garlic cloves,
  crushed

2 tablespoons tahini

2 tablespoons olive oil,
  plus extra to garnish

2 tablespoons freshly
  squeezed lemon juice

garlic sprouts, to
  garnish (optional)

**GOATS'
CHEESE WITH
CARAMELIZED
RED ONION
AND BEETROOT**

450 g (14½ oz) red
  onions, thinly sliced

1 tablespoon olive oil

1 tablespoon caster
  sugar

1 tablespoon red wine
  vinegar

450 g (14½ oz) cooked
  beetroot, diced

200 g (7 oz) soft goats'
  cheese

rosemary leaves,
  to garnish

I like to use rosemary-flavoured bread to make the crunchy bases and contrasting toppings (that also make good dips) for these pretty, tasty morsels.

1 First make the bruschette. Slice the bread, then brush each slice on both sides with olive oil. If you're using a plain baguette, sprinkle each piece on both sides with a good pinch of crushed dried rosemary. Place the bread on a baking sheet and bake in a preheated oven, 150°C (300°F), Gas Mark 2, for about 20 minutes until crisp. Cool on wire racks. The bruschette can be made up to 1 week in advance and kept in an airtight container.

2 Next make the toppings. For the aubergine caviar, prick the aubergines in several places and cook them under a very hot grill for 25–30 minutes until soft and well charred. Cool slightly, then peel off the skin and whiz the aubergine to a pale cream with the garlic, tahini, the 2 tablespoons of olive oil and the lemon juice. Season with salt and pepper and chill until required.

3 For the goats' cheese with caramelized red onion and beetroot, cook the onions in the olive oil in a large saucepan, covered, for about 15 minutes until they're very tender, stirring them every 5 minutes. Add the sugar, wine vinegar and beetroot, then simmer gently, uncovered, for 10–15 minutes. Remove from the heat, season with salt and pepper and cool.

4 For the chestnut pâté, put the chestnuts into a food processor with the butter, garlic and lemon juice. Whiz to a fairly smooth purée and season with salt and pepper.

CHESTNUT PÂTÉ

- **200 g (7 oz) vacuum-packed whole peeled chestnuts**
- **15 g (½ oz) butter**
- **1 garlic clove, crushed**
- **2 tablespoons freshly squeezed lemon juice**
- **paprika (or finely chopped small sweet red peppers from a jar) and thyme sprigs, to garnish**

5 To assemble the bruschette, spread one-third with aubergine caviar and garnish with a drizzle of olive oil and a few garlic sprouts, if liked. Spread another third with goats' cheese, and top with caramelized onion and beetroot and a little rosemary. Spread the remainder with chestnut pâté and a dusting of paprika or sweet red peppers and thyme sprigs.

Falafel with Lemon Sauce

SERVES 4

275 g (9 oz) dried
  chickpeas

1 small onion, roughly
  chopped

15 g (½ oz) fresh
  coriander

2 garlic cloves, roughly
  chopped

1 tablespoon ground
  cumin

½ teaspoon bicarbonate
  of soda

1½ teaspoons salt

2 tablespoons gram
  (chickpea) flour

rapeseed oil, for
  shallow-frying

LEMON SAUCE

4 tablespoons natural
  yogurt (dairy or vegan)

4 tablespoons good-
  quality mayonnaise
  (dairy or vegan)

grated rind of ½ lemon

1–2 tablespoons lemon
  juice

TO SERVE

warm halved pitta
  bread

shredded lettuce, sliced
  tomato, cucumber and
  onion, mint sprigs
  and grated carrot
  (optional)

These freeze well before or after frying, so if you like them it's worth making a larger batch: use a 500 g (1 lb) packet of chickpeas and double everything else.

1 Put the chickpeas in a saucepan and cover with lots of water. Bring to the boil and boil for 2 minutes, then leave to soak for 1–2 hours. (Alternatively, just soak them overnight.) Drain.

2 Put the drained chickpeas into a food processor with the onion, coriander, garlic, cumin, bicarbonate of soda and salt, and whiz until the ingredients are finely ground and hold together.

3 Take a small handful of the mixture and squeeze it between your palms to extract any excess liquid. Shape it into a small flat cake. Repeat until you've used up all the mixture, then coat the falafels lightly in gram flour.

4 Shallow-fry the falafel in hot rapeseed oil until brown and crisp on all sides. Drain on kitchen paper.

5 To make the sauce, simply mix all the ingredients together. Serve the falafel with the warm pitta bread: people can fill the pitta halves with a selection of hot falafels, salad and lemon sauce.

Mushroom Tempura with Aïoli

SERVES 4

500 g (1 lb) mixed wild
  mushrooms, torn into
  bite-sized pieces

rapeseed oil, for
  deep-frying

aïoli (garlic mayonnaise),
  to serve

TEMPURA BATTER

100 g (3½ oz) plain flour

200 g (7 oz) cornflour

3 teaspoons baking
  powder

200 ml (7 fl oz)
  sparkling water

salt

I love these best as an informal kitchen feast so you can eat each batch as it's ready. The tempura are crisp, light and golden, gorgeous dipped in aïoli (garlic mayonnaise).

1 Just before you want to serve the mushrooms, heat sufficient oil for deep-frying in a deep-fat fryer to 180–190°C (356–374°F), or until a cube of bread browns in 30 seconds.

2 While the oil is heating, make the batter. Put the flour, cornflour and baking powder into a bowl with some salt. Pour in the water and stir the mixture quickly with a fork or chopstick until smooth.

3 Dip pieces of mushroom into the batter, then put them into the hot oil for 1–2 minutes until they are golden brown and very crisp. Lift them out on to kitchen paper. You will need to do a number of batches, but the first ones will keep crisp while you do the rest.

4 Pile the tempura on 1 sharing plate or divide between 4 individual plates and serve immediately with the aïoli.

Red Bean Cakes with Guacamole

SERVES 4

2 × 425 g (14 oz) cans red kidney beans

2 large spring onions, roughly chopped

2 garlic cloves, crushed

2 tablespoons tomato ketchup

½–1 teaspoon ground cumin

½ teaspoon chilli powder

salt and pepper

COATING AND FRYING

4 tablespoons cornflour

4–5 tablespoons water

8 tablespoons dried breadcrumbs

2–4 tablespoons olive oil

GUACAMOLE

2 ripe avocados

2 spring onions, chopped

1 tomato, chopped

½ packet (14 g) fresh coriander

juice of 1 lime

1 chilli, deseeded and finely chopped

This healthy snack has a lovely mixture of colours, flavours and textures, and is very easy to make.

1 Drain the beans in a sieve and blot thoroughly with kitchen paper so that they're fairly dry.

2 Put the beans into a food processor with the spring onions, garlic, tomato ketchup, cumin and chilli powder. Process until everything has combined and season with salt and pepper.

3 Form the mixture into 8 even-sized flat cakes, pressing them firmly together.

4 For the coating, mix the cornflour with 4 tablespoons of the water, then carefully add enough of the remaining water just to loosen the mixture but not make it sloppy: it needs to remain sticky, but not stiff.

5 Dip the bean cakes first in the cornflour mixture, then into the dried breadcrumbs, coating them all over.

6 Heat 1–2 tablespoons of the olive oil in a frying pan – use just enough to grease the pan lightly – and fry the cakes gently in batches, first on one side and then on the other, until they are crisp and lightly browned. Add more oil to the pan as needed.

7 While the bean cakes are frying, make the guacamole. Remove the skin and stones from the avocados and chop the flesh into chunky pieces. In a bowl, mix the avocado pieces with the spring onions, tomato, coriander, lime juice and enough chilli for your taste, then season with salt and pepper.

8 Serve the bean cakes with the guacamole.

Plantain Bhajis and Coconut Chutney

SERVES 4
(MAKES ABOUT
20 BHAJIS)

125 g (4 oz) gram
(chickpea) flour

½–1 teaspoon dried red
chilli flakes

½ teaspoon turmeric

2 teaspoons ground
coriander

2 teaspoons ground
cumin

2 teaspoons cumin
seeds

150–200 ml (5–7 fl oz)
sparkling water

rapeseed oil, for frying

1 plantain, about 325 g
(11 oz)

salt

COCONUT
CHUTNEY

75 g (3 oz) fresh coconut
(about one-quarter of
a coconut), grated

20 g (¾ oz) packet fresh
coriander

juice and grated rind
of 1 lime

1 teaspoon black
mustard seeds

It's easy to find plantains in Indian, African or Caribbean shops and many large supermarkets. You can also use unripe banana to make this mouthwatering snack or starter.

1 First make the chutney. Put the grated coconut, fresh coriander and lime juice and rind into a food processor and whiz until combined. Stir in the mustard seeds and, if necessary, a little cold water to make a soft, creamy consistency. Set aside.

2 Mix the gram flour, chilli flakes, turmeric, ground coriander, ground cumin, cumin seeds and some salt with enough sparkling water to make a batter that will coat the back of a spoon.

3 When you are ready to serve the bhajis, heat 2.5 cm (1 inch) of oil in a deep frying pan. Peel the plantain and cut it diagonally into slices about 1 cm (½ inch) thick.

4 Dip a slice of plantain into the batter, then put it into the hot oil – it should sizzle immediately. Repeat with several more slices until the frying pan is full. Turn the slices when the underside is golden brown and crisp.

5 When the bhajis are done, remove them with a slotted spoon on to crumpled kitchen paper. Serve at once in batches, with the chutney – or keep the first bhajis warm while you fry the rest, then serve all at once, hot and crisp.

Salsify Fritters with Caper Cream

SERVES 4

700 g (1 lb 7 oz) salsify
  (scorzonera)

2 tablespoons lemon
  juice

1 tablespoon olive oil

1 tablespoon red wine
  vinegar

salt and pepper

2 large eggs, beaten

flour, for coating

75 g (3 oz) dried
  breadcrumbs

rapeseed oil, for
  deep-frying

lemon wedges, to serve

CAPER CREAM

2 tablespoons
  mayonnaise

2 tablespoons crème
  fraîche

1 tablespoon capers,
  rinsed

It's getting easier to find salsify (or scorzonera), but if you're unsuccessful bring some canned salsify back next time you visit France – it's available in any supermarket.

1 Wearing gloves to protect your hands (the juice can stain), peel the salsify under a cold running tap, cut it into about 3 cm (1¼ inch) lengths and put in a saucepan of water containing 1 tablespoon of the lemon juice. Don't worry if you can't remove all the skin – some tiny flecks don't matter.

2 Boil the pieces in the water for about 10 minutes, or until tender, then drain and add the remaining lemon juice, the olive oil, red wine vinegar and some salt and pepper. Leave to cool.

3 Meanwhile, make the caper cream. Mix the mayonnaise with the crème fraîche and capers and season to taste with salt and pepper.

4 Dip each piece of salsify into the beaten eggs, then into flour, then into the eggs again and finally into the breadcrumbs, to coat all over.

5 Heat the oil to 180–190°C (356–374°F), or until a cube of bread browns in 30 seconds, and deep-fry the coated pieces for about 3 minutes, or until they are crisp and golden brown. Drain on kitchen paper and serve at once, garnished with lemon wedges and accompanied by the caper cream.

Red Pepper Hummus with Paprika

SERVES 4

2 garlic cloves

410 g (13½ oz) can
  chickpeas, drained

½ × 325 g (11 oz) jar
  whole sweet red
  peppers, drained

1 teaspoon honey

Tabasco sauce, to taste

¼–½ teaspoon smoked
  paprika

pepper

warm or griddled pitta
  bread, to serve

*A great variation on traditional hummus. I bet you can make it in
less time that it takes to go to the shop and buy some!*

1 Whiz the garlic cloves in a food processor until chopped,
then add the chickpeas, red peppers and honey and whiz
again. Stir in the Tabasco and smoked paprika to taste.

2 Turn the mixture on to a flat plate and smooth the
surface. Grind some black pepper coarsely over the top
and serve with strips of warm or griddled pitta bread.

Lemon-glazed and Seared Haloumi

SERVES 4

2 × 250 g (8 oz) **packets haloumi cheese, drained**

4 tablespoons lemon juice

2 tablespoons clear honey

HERB SALAD

250 g (8 oz) **mixed baby leaves**

2 tablespoons olive oil

salt and pepper

This could be an emergency meal – you could probably find all the ingredients in your local corner shop – but it's elegant and delicious. Try it with the Herby Couscous with Red Chilli on page 128.

1 Cut the haloumi into slices about 5 mm (¼ inch) thick. Put them on a plate in a single layer.

2 Mix the lemon juice with the honey and pour over the haloumi, turning the slices so that they are coated all over. Set aside for at least 1 hour.

3 When you are ready to serve, make the salad. Toss the leaves with the olive oil and salt and pepper and divide between 4 plates.

4 Put the slices of haloumi into a dry frying pan over a moderate heat, reserving any liquid. Fry the slices on one side until golden brown, then flip them over and fry the second side. This is a very quick process as they cook fast. When the second sides are done, pour in any remaining liquid and let it bubble up until it has mostly evaporated and becomes a sweet glaze.

5 Arrange the slices of haloumi on top of the salad and serve at once.

Baby Yorkshire Puddings

MAKES 24

50 g (2 oz) **plain flour**

1 **egg**

75 ml (3 fl oz) **milk**

75 ml (3 fl oz) **water**

olive oil

salt and pepper

horseradish sauce,
   to serve

NUT ROAST

50 g (2 oz) **almonds**

25 g (1 oz) **wholemeal**
   bread

50 g (2 oz) **cheese,**
   grated

50 g (2 oz) **onion,**
   roughly chopped

½ teaspoon **dried mixed**
   herbs

1 tablespoon **shoyu**
   or tamari

A friend was raving about the mini Yorkshire puddings with beef she'd had at a party, so I thought I'd try them with nut roast, and they're always a big hit.

1 First prepare the batter for the Yorkshire puddings. Sift the flour into a bowl with a pinch of salt. Make a well in the centre, break the egg into it and mix to a paste, then gradually draw in the flour. Mix the milk with the water, then stir the mixture into the bowl, but don't overbeat. Transfer the batter to a jug, so that it will be easy to pour it into the baking tins, and leave to rest for 30 minutes. This allows the starch to swell, giving a lighter result.

2 Meanwhile, prepare the nut roast. Put all the ingredients into a food processor and whiz until you have a smooth mixture that holds together. Form it into 24 cocktail sausages, coat them all over with olive oil and place on a baking sheet.

3 Use 2 × 12-hole nonstick mini-muffin tins, each hole measuring 1.5 cm (¾ inch) across and about 1.5 cm (¾ inch) deep, for the Yorkshire puddings. Put ½ teaspoon olive oil into each hole and put the tins into a preheated oven, 220°C (425°F), Gas Mark 7. The oil needs to heated for 10 minutes before you put the batter in.

4 Put the nut-roast sausages in the oven at this point (they will take longer to cook than the Yorkshire puddings) and roast for about 15 minutes, or until brown and crisp.

5 When the oil in the muffin tins is smoking hot, quickly pour the batter into each hole, filling the tins about two-thirds full. Bake for 10 minutes, until the puddings are puffed up and golden. Pop them out of the tins and cool on a wire rack.

6 When you want to serve the Yorkshire puddings, put them on a heatproof serving dish and place a nut-roast sausage on top of each one. Put them in a preheated oven, 220°C (425°F), Gas Mark 7, for 4–5 minutes, until hot and puffy. Serve immediately with horseradish sauce.

Rosemary Sorbet

SERVES 4

450 ml (¾ pint) water

150 g (5 oz) caster sugar

5 rosemary sprigs

250 ml (8 fl oz) white wine

4 tablespoons freshly squeezed lemon juice

TO DECORATE

a few small sprigs and flowers of rosemary (optional)

This is wonderful as a refresher between courses. We had it at my daughter's wedding reception on a balmy midsummer evening and it went down a treat.

1 Put the water and sugar into a saucepan with 4 of the rosemary sprigs and bring to the boil. Once the sugar has dissolved, remove from the heat, cover and set aside to cool and infuse the flavour of the rosemary.

2 Remove the rosemary from the cooled syrup and stir in the wine and lemon juice. Chop the remaining rosemary sprig and stir it in.

3 Pour the mixture into a shallow container and freeze for about 2 hours, or until firm, scraping down the sides and whisking as it solidifies. Alternatively, freeze in an ice-cream maker until the mixture is soft and slushy, then transfer to a plastic container and freeze until required.

4 Remove the sorbet from the freezer about 15 minutes before you want to serve it, then scoop it into bowls and decorate with rosemary sprigs and flowers, if liked.

Scones with Homemade Strawberry Jam

MAKES ABOUT
10 SCONES AND
400 G (13 OZ)
JAM

250 g (8 oz) self-raising flour, plus extra for dusting

80 g (3 oz) butter

1 tablespoon golden caster sugar (optional)

125 ml (4 fl oz) milk

clotted cream, to serve

STRAWBERRY
JAM

500 g (1 lb) strawberries (squashy ones are fine), hulled

250 g (8 oz) sugar

1 teaspoon butter

1 tablespoon lemon juice

Who can resist homemade scones and jam? Make the jam in advance, and the scones at the last minute and enjoy them warm.

1 First make the jam. Put the strawberries into a saucepan and mash roughly. Cook them over a medium heat for 5–6 minutes, until the juices run and thicken a little. Add the sugar and stir over a gentle heat until dissolved, then turn the heat up and boil gently until the mixture thickens and sticks to a spoon, about 20 minutes, stirring often.

2 Stir in the butter, which will disperse the foam, then add the lemon juice. Put the jam into a serving bowl, or sterilized jar (sterilize the jar by running it through the hottest dishwasher cycle or filling it with 1 cm/½ inch water and microwaving it for 3 minutes).

3 To make the scones, put the flour into a bowl or food processor, add the butter and rub with your fingertips, or pulse, until the mixture resembles fine breadcrumbs. Add the sugar, if using, and the milk, keeping a little milk back at first in case you don't need all of it, and mix gently to a soft, slightly sticky dough.

4 Turn the mixture out on to a lightly floured board and pat it gently to a thickness of 2.5 cm (1 inch).

5 Using a 5.5-cm (2¼-inch) round cutter, stamp the scones straight out of the dough, without twisting the cutter, and place them on a baking sheet. Gently press the trimmings together and use them to make another 1–2 scones.

6 Dust the scones with flour and bake in a preheated oven, 220°C (425°F), Gas Mark 7, for 10–12 minutes, until risen and golden brown. Cool slightly and serve as soon as possible, with clotted cream and strawberry jam.

Everyday Meals

Jewelled Pilaf

SERVES 4

1 tablespoon olive oil

1 onion, finely chopped

½ teaspoon cumin
   seeds

3 cardamom pods,
   lightly crushed

3 star anise

½ cinnamon stick

1 bay leaf

250 g (8 oz) Basmati
   and wild rice

500 ml (17 fl oz)
   vegetable stock

250 g (8 oz) frozen
   edamame beans

50 g (2 oz) pine nuts

seeds from ½–1
   pomegranate

4 tablespoons roughly
   chopped flat leaf
   parsley

salt and pepper

Fresh-tasting, protein-rich edamame beans, podded and frozen, are available from health shops and supermarkets. The mixture of Basmati and wild rice that I like to use is also widely available.

1 Heat the olive oil in a heavy-based saucepan, add the onion and cook, covered, for 5 minutes, until lightly browned.

2 Add the cumin seeds, cardamom pods, star anise and cinnamon and stir over the heat for 1 minute, then add the bay leaf and rice. Stir for another minute, then pour in the vegetable stock.

3 Bring the rice to the boil, cover, and turn the heat right down. Leave to cook very gently and undisturbed for 20–25 minutes, until all the water has been absorbed and the rice is tender. Remove from the heat and leave to stand, still covered, for 5 minutes.

4 Meanwhile cook or microwave the edamame beans according to the directions on the packet. Drain and set aside.

5 Toast the pine nuts by putting them into a dry saucepan and stirring over a moderate heat for 4–5 minutes, or until they turn golden brown in places and smell toasty. Turn them out of the pan on to a plate to cool.

6 Stir the rice gently with a fork and add most of the beans, pomegranate seeds, toasted pine nuts and chopped parsley, reserving some of each to garnish. Season with salt and plenty of pepper.

7 Serve the pilaf heaped up on a warm serving dish, scattered with the remaining beans, pomegranate seeds, pine nuts and parsley, to give a jewelled effect.

Spaghetti with Lentil Bolognese

SERVES 4

225–350 g (7½–11½ oz) spaghetti

1 tablespoon olive oil

LENTIL
BOLOGNESE
SAUCE

225 g (7½ oz) cooked whole green lentils, cooking liquid reserved, or 2 × 400 g (13 oz) cans green lentils

2 tablespoons olive oil

2 onions, chopped

2 garlic cloves, crushed

2 celery sticks, chopped

2 carrots, finely diced

400 g (13 oz) can chopped tomatoes

salt and pepper

grated Parmesan-style cheese, to serve (optional)

My daughter and her boyfriend lived on this when they were at medical school. Now they're married with a young family, but it's still one of their favourite dishes!

1 Make the sauce. If you are using canned lentils, drain them and keep the liquid.

2 Heat the olive oil in a saucepan, add the onions and cook gently for 5 minutes without browning, then add the garlic, celery and carrots. Simmer, covered, for 15 minutes, until the vegetables are tender.

3 Stir in the lentils, chopped tomatoes, salt and pepper, and a little of the reserved liquid to make a thick, soft consistency. Simmer for about 10 minutes, adding more liquid if necessary.

4 Half-fill a large saucepan with water, add 1 teaspoon salt and bring to the boil. Add the spaghetti and simmer for about 10 minutes, until just tender. Drain the spaghetti, then return it to the saucepan with the olive oil, and pepper, to taste.

5 Make sure the spaghetti is hot, then turn it out on to a hot serving dish and pour the sauce on top. Hand round grated Parmesan-style cheese, if liked.

Quick Thai Curry with Jasmine Rice

SERVES 4

2–4 tablespoons green
Thai curry paste

400 ml (14 fl oz) can
organic coconut milk

150 g (5 oz) untrimmed
baby carrots, peeled

200 g (7 oz) baby
sweetcorn, halved
diagonally

150 g (5 oz) sugar snap
peas, trimmed

2–3 pak choi (1 packet),
quartered

a squeeze of lime juice

salt and pepper

JASMINE RICE

250 g (8 oz) jasmine rice

500 ml (17 fl oz) water

TO GARNISH

1 red chilli, deseeded
and sliced

2 tablespoons chopped
coriander

4 tablespoons crushed
salted peanuts

*So quick to make, and so tasty! Most large supermarkets sell tubs
of vegetarian green Thai curry paste. It keeps for ages in the fridge.*

1 First cook the jasmine rice. Put it into a saucepan with
the water, bring to the boil, then cover and cook over a
very gentle heat for about 20 minutes, or the length of
time advised on the packet.

2 To make the curry, put 2 tablespoons of the Thai
curry paste into a large saucepan and stir over the heat
for 1–2 minutes, gradually adding the remaining paste
to taste, until it smells aromatic, then pour in the
coconut milk.

3 Add the carrots, baby sweetcorn, sugar snap peas and
bring to the boil. Cover and cook gently for 10–15 minutes,
or until the vegetables are tender. Add the pak choi
5 minutes before the end of the cooking time.

4 Add the lime juice to freshen the flavour, and season
with salt and pepper.

5 Fork through the rice, then serve it on individual warm
plates, along with the curry. Top each serving with a little
red chilli, chopped coriander and crushed peanuts.

Mediterranean Stuffed Peppers

SERVES 4

4 mixed peppers, such as Ramano

200 g (7 oz) feta cheese, roughly crumbled

16 cherry tomatoes, halved

8 heaped teaspoons pesto

CAULIFLOWER MASH

1 cauliflower, trimmed and cut into florets

25 g (1 oz) butter

salt and pepper

These peppers are an established favourite in my family. The cauliflower mash turns them into a light meal, or you could try the Herby Couscous with Red Chilli on page 128.

1 Halve the peppers, cutting right through the stems if you can. Trim the insides and rinse away all the seeds. Put the peppers in a roasting tin or large, shallow casserole dish. Mix together the feta, cherry tomatoes and pesto, then divide the mixture between the peppers.

2 Bake in a preheated oven, 200°C (400°F), Gas Mark 6, for 30 minutes, or until the tops are charring and the insides are full of luscious juice.

3 Meanwhile, make the cauliflower mash. Bring 5 cm (2 inches) depth of water to the boil in a large saucepan. Add the cauliflower, bring back to the boil, cover and cook for 5–6 minutes, until the cauliflower is tender. Drain well.

4 Put the cauliflower into a food processor with the butter and salt and pepper and whiz to a smooth, thick mixture. Return to the saucepan and reheat gently, stirring so that the mash doesn't catch. Serve with the peppers.

Penne Arrabbiata

SERVES 4

4 litres (7 pints) water

3 tablespoons olive oil

1 large onion, chopped

2 cloves garlic, chopped

½–1 teaspoon dried red
chilli flakes

2 × 400 g (13 oz) cans
tomatoes, coarsely
chopped, with juice

400 g (13 oz) penne, or
other tubular pasta
such as rigatoni

salt and pepper

basil leaves, to garnish

Parmesan-style cheese,
cut into flakes, to
serve (optional)

*Easy and delicious. You can make it as hot as you like by varying
the amount of red chilli flakes.*

1 For cooking the penne or other pasta, pour the water
into a large pan and place over a high heat.

2 Warm 2 tablespoons of the olive oil in a saucepan over
a moderate heat, add the onion, cover and cook for about
5 minutes, until tender. Add the garlic and chilli and cook
for a further 2 minutes.

3 Pour in the chopped tomatoes with their juice and cook,
uncovered, for 10–15 minutes, until the excess tomato
liquid has evaporated and the sauce has reduced. Season
with salt and pepper and keep warm.

4 Meanwhile, when the water in the pan reaches a rolling
boil, drop in the pasta. Bring back to the boil, give the
pasta a quick stir, then let the water boil steadily until the
pasta is *al dente* – tender but not soft right through. Bite
a piece to check.

5 Drain the pasta but leave some water clinging to it, and
return it to the hot pan with the remaining olive oil and
a good seasoning of salt and pepper. Toss the pasta to coat
it with the oil.

6 Add the sauce to the pasta and toss well, making sure
the pasta is well coated with the sauce. Garnish with basil
leaves and serve at once, with flakes of Parmesan-style
cheese, if liked.

Grilled Polenta and Roasted Tomatoes

SERVES 4

1.2 litres (2 pints) water

250 g (8 oz) dry polenta

125 g (4 oz) Parmesan-style or strong Cheddar cheese, grated

olive oil, for brushing

salt and pepper

ROASTED TOMATOES

1.1 kg (2¼ lb) tomatoes on the vine

2 tablespoons olive oil

2 tablespoons balsamic vinegar

8–10 thyme sprigs

You can grill the polenta or cook it on a barbecue. For a vegan version, try swapping the cheese for lots of chopped parsley or black olives.

1 First make the polenta. Bring the water to the boil in a large saucepan and add the polenta to the water in a thin, steady stream, stirring all the time. Let it simmer for 5–10 minutes, stirring from time to time, or until it's very thick and leaves the sides of the pan.

2 Remove from the heat, stir in the Parmesan-style cheese or Cheddar and season with salt and pepper. Turn the mixture on to a lightly oiled baking sheet or large plate, and spread and press it out to a depth of 5–7 mm (¼–⅓ inch). Leave to become completely cold and firm.

3 To roast the tomatoes, put them, complete with their vines, into a roasting tin. Drizzle with the olive oil and balsamic vinegar, scatter with a little salt and the thyme sprigs and place in the top of a preheated oven, 200°C (400°F), Gas Mark 6, for 30–40 minutes, or until tender and lightly browned.

4 Just before you want to serve the meal, cut the polenta into manageable pieces, brush lightly with olive oil and cook under a preheated grill on both sides, until crisp and lightly charred. Serve at once, with the tomatoes.

Bubble-and-squeak Cakes

SERVES 4

1 kg (2 lb) potatoes, peeled and cut into even-sized pieces

40 g (1½ oz) butter

1 sweetheart or similar cabbage, shredded

6 spring onions, finely chopped

2–3 tablespoons wholemeal flour

olive oil, for shallow-frying

salt and pepper

BEETROOT RELISH

2 cooked beetroots, peeled and diced

2 tablespoons finely chopped onion

1 tablespoon clear honey

1 tablespoon cider vinegar

TO GARNISH

olive oil

dill sprigs

I like bubble-and-squeak and I love beetroot: here my 'shot' of beetroot is provided by a tasty relish. This is a gorgeous combination.

1 First make the beetroot relish. Put the beetroots into a bowl, stir in the onion, honey and cider vinegar, and season with salt and pepper. Set aside for at least 30 minutes until needed – this relish improves with keeping: it's fine to make it several hours in advance if convenient.

2 Meanwhile, cover the potatoes in boiling water and cook for about 20 minutes, or until tender. Drain and mash with the butter.

3 Put the cabbage into 2 cm (1 inch) of boiling water, cover and cook for about 6 minutes, until tender. Drain well, then add the cabbage to the potatoes, along with the spring onions and salt and pepper.

4 Form the mixture into 4 large, flat cakes. Just before you want to serve the bubble-and-squeak, coat the cakes all over in the wholemeal flour, then immediately shallow-fry them in sizzling-hot olive oil until browned and crisp on both sides.

5 Serve at once, topping each cake with a spoonful of beetroot relish, a drizzle of olive oil and dill sprigs.

Leek and Parsley Risotto

SERVES 4

1 tablespoon olive oil

1 onion, chopped

1 celery stick, finely chopped

1.2 litres (2 pints) vegetable stock

2 garlic cloves, crushed

350 g (11½ oz) carnaroli or risotto rice

2 wine glasses of dry white vermouth or white wine

250 g (8 oz) leeks, trimmed, cleaned and cut into 2 cm (¾ inch) lengths

50 g (2 oz) butter

75 g (3 oz) Parmesan-style cheese, grated

4 tablespoons chopped parsley

salt and pepper

Everyone loves risotto and this is a particular favourite. You can use other vegetables, too: try asparagus tips, peas and mint, or butternut squash and sage.

1 Heat the olive oil in a large saucepan, add the onion and celery, stir, and then cover and cook gently, without browning, for 7–8 minutes.

2 Meanwhile, heat the vegetable stock (you can use a stock cube or bouillon powder for this) in another pan, and keep it keep warm.

3 Add the garlic and rice to the pan containing the onions and celery and stir well. Add half the vermouth or wine and stir continuously over the heat until it has bubbled away. Repeat the process with remaining the vermouth or wine.

4 Add a ladleful of the hot stock, and when nearly all of that has bubbled away, add another ladleful, and so on, for 5–10 minutes, then add the leeks.

5 Continue adding the stock, stirring continuously, for another 5–10 minutes, or until the rice is cooked to your liking and most, or all, of the stock has been added.

6 Remove from the heat, season with salt and pepper, and add the butter and Parmesan-style cheese. Cover and leave to stand for 2 minutes, then beat in the chopped parsley. Check the seasoning, and serve at once.

Three-bean Chilli with Peppers

SERVES 4

- 1 tablespoon olive oil
- 1 onion, chopped
- 2 garlic cloves, finely chopped
- 1 green chilli, deseeded and chopped
- 1 red, 1 yellow and 1 green pepper, cored, deseeded and chopped
- 410 g (13½ oz) can borlotti beans
- 410 g (13½ oz) can red kidney beans
- 410 g (13½ oz) can pinto beans
- 400 g (13 oz) can chopped tomatoes
- Tabasco sauce (optional)
- salt and pepper

You don't need meat to make a great chilli! Try this: it's easy to prepare and lovely to look at and eat, with its colourful peppers and contrasting beans.

1 Heat the olive oil in a large saucepan, add the onion, cover and cook gently without browning for 5 minutes. Add the garlic, chilli and peppers, stir, then cover and cook for a further 15–20 minutes, or until the peppers are tender.

2 Add all the beans, together with their liquid, and the tomatoes. Stir and bring to a simmer, then cook over a gentle heat for about 10 minutes, until the vegetables are very tender.

3 Taste and season with salt and pepper, and a dash of Tabasco if you think the chilli needs to be a bit hotter, then serve.

Cheese and Parsley Fritters

SERVES 4

600 ml (1 pint) milk

1 small onion, stuck
with 1 clove

1 bay leaf

100 g (3½ oz) semolina

100 g (3½ oz) Cheddar
cheese, grated

1–2 tablespoons
chopped parsley

a good pinch of cayenne
pepper

1 large egg, beaten with
1 tablespoon water

dried breadcrumbs,
for coating

olive oil, for shallow-
frying

salt and pepper

TO GARNISH

lemon slices

parsley sprigs

*If you like these fritters, it's worth making a double quantity and
freezing some. To use, just shallow-fry from frozen. Or fry before
freezing and heat through in a moderate oven.*

1 Bring the milk, onion and bay leaf to the boil in a large
saucepan, then remove from the heat, cover and leave to
infuse for 10–15 minutes.

2 Remove and discard the onion and bay leaf. Return the
milk to the boil, then gradually sprinkle the semolina over
the top, stirring all the time.

3 Simmer for about 5 minutes, stirring often, to cook
the semolina, then remove from the heat and beat in the
grated Cheddar, chopped parsley and cayenne pepper,
and season with salt and pepper.

4 Spread the mixture out to a depth of about 1 cm
(½ inch) on an oiled plate or baking sheet. Smooth the
surface and allow to cool completely.

5 Cut the mixture into squares or triangles. Dip first
into the beaten egg, then the dried breadcrumbs, to coat
thoroughly. Shallow-fry in hot olive oil until crisp on
both sides, then drain the fritters well on kitchen paper.

6 Garnish with slices of lemon and parsley sprigs, and
serve immediately.

Vegetable Curry

SERVES 4

50 g (2 oz) ghee or butter

1 large onion, chopped

2 garlic cloves, crushed

1 bay leaf

3 teaspoons ground
coriander

3 teaspoons ground
cumin

1–2 teaspoons grated
fresh root ginger

¼ teaspoon chilli
powder

225 g (7½ oz) canned
tomatoes

1 teaspoon sea salt

pepper

575 ml (18 fl oz) water

350 g (11½ oz) carrots,
sliced

350 g (11½ oz) potatoes,
peeled and cut into
even-sized chunks

125 g (4 oz) peas

chopped fresh
coriander, to garnish

Serve this with hot brown or white Basmati rice. Some poppadums and mango chutney are nice with it, too.

1 Heat the ghee or butter in a large saucepan, add the onion and fry gently for 7–8 minutes without browning. Add the garlic, bay leaf, ground coriander and cumin, grated ginger and chilli powder, and stir for 1–2 minutes.

2 Mix in the tomatoes, salt and a grinding of pepper, and pour in the water. Simmer for 5–10 minutes.

3 Add the carrots and potatoes to the tomato mixture and simmer gently for 15–25 minutes, until the vegetables are almost tender, then put in the peas and simmer for a further 5 minutes.

4 Check the seasoning, then scatter with chopped fresh coriander and serve.

Favourite Macaroni Cheese

SERVES 4

350 g (11½ oz) short macaroni

3 tablespoons olive oil

3 tablespoons plain flour

600 ml (1 pint) milk or unsweetened soya milk

150 g (5 oz) Boursin cheese with herbs and garlic or black pepper (optional)

1–2 heaped teaspoons Dijon mustard

2–3 tablespoons capers, rinsed and drained

250 g (8 oz) strong Cheddar cheese, grated

freshly grated nutmeg

250 g (8 oz) cherry tomatoes, halved

salt and pepper

This is a very tasty version of macaroni cheese. The Boursin cheese is a luxury touch that can be omitted but makes the dish particularly creamy and delicious.

1 Bring a large pan of lightly salted water to the boil, put in the macaroni, give it a stir and boil steadily for 8–10 minutes, or until *al dente*. Drain into a colander.

2 Pour the olive oil into another large pan and add the flour. Stir over the heat for 1–2 minutes, until smooth and combined, then add the milk, a quarter at a time, whisking well after each addition, to make a thick, smooth sauce.

3 Remove from the heat and stir in the Boursin, if using, the mustard, capers, most of the grated Cheddar – leave a handful to sprinkle over the top – and the cooked and drained macaroni.

4 Season with with grated nutmeg, salt and pepper, then gently stir in the cherry tomatoes.

5 Turn the mixture into a shallow ovenproof dish and scatter with the remaining Cheddar. Bake in a preheated oven, 200°C (400°F), Gas Mark 6, for 30 minutes, until bubbly and golden.

Lentil Shepherd's Pie

SERVES 4

- 1.1 kg (2¼ lb) potatoes, peeled and cut into even-sized pieces
- 2 tablespoons olive oil
- 2 large onions, chopped
- 2 garlic cloves, crushed
- 400 g (13 oz) can chopped tomatoes
- 410 g (13½ oz) can whole green lentils, drained
- 50 g (2 oz) sun-dried tomatoes, chopped
- 1 tablespoon tomato ketchup
- 15 g (½ oz) butter
- 200 g (7 oz) smoked Wensleydale or Cheddar cheese, crumbled or grated
- salt and pepper
- cooked petit pois or kale, to serve

This is as popular with meat-eaters as it is with vegetarians; I think it's the smoked cheese that adds the satisfying 'extra something' that really appeals.

1 Put the potatoes in a saucepan, cover with water and bring to the boil. Boil for about 20 minutes until tender.

2 Meanwhile, heat the olive oil in a large saucepan. Add the chopped onions, cover, and cook gently for 15 minutes, or until very tender, lightly browned and sweet. Remove from the heat and add the garlic, chopped tomatoes, lentils, sun-dried tomatoes and tomato ketchup. Season with salt and pepper.

3 Drain the boiled potatoes, reserving the water, then mash with the butter and enough reserved water to make a creamy consistency. Stir in two-thirds of the Wensleydale or Cheddar.

4 Pour the lentil mixture into a shallow casserole dish and spread the potato on top. Scatter with the remaining cheese and bake in a preheated oven, 200°C (400°F), Gas Mark 6, for 40 minutes, until golden brown. Serve with petit pois or kale.

Omelette Cannelloni

SERVES 4

750 g (1½ lb) spinach, washed

125 g (4 oz) low-fat soft cream cheese

8 tablespoons grated Parmesan-style cheese

freshly grated nutmeg

4 eggs

2 tablespoons water

1 tablespoon olive oil

salt and pepper

If you want something light but satisfying, and pretty to look at, try this. It makes a lovely lunch or supper dish.

1 Put the spinach with just the water clinging to the leaves into a large saucepan, cover and cook for 6–7 minutes, or until tender. Drain well.

2 Add the cream cheese to the spinach along with 4 tablespoons of the Parmesan-style cheese. Mix well and season with salt, pepper and grated nutmeg. Set aside.

3 Whisk the eggs with the water and some salt and pepper. Brush a frying pan (preferably nonstick) with a little of the olive oil and heat, then pour in enough of the egg – about 2 tablespoons – to make a small omelette. Cook for a few seconds, until it is set, then lift out on to a plate. Continue in this way until you have made about 8 small omelettes, piling them on top of each other.

4 Spoon a little of the spinach mixture on to the edge of one of the omelettes, roll it up and place in a shallow gratin dish. Fill the remaining omelettes in the same way, until all the spinach mixture is used, placing them snugly side by side in the dish. Sprinkle with the remaining Parmesan-style cheese and bake in a preheated oven, 190°C (375°F), Gas Mark 5, for about 25 minutes, or until bubbling and golden brown on top. Serve hot.

Vegetarian Sausages with Garlic Mash

SERVES 4

500 g (1 lb) vegetarian
sausages

GARLIC MASH

1 kg (2 lb) potatoes,
peeled and cut into
even-sized pieces

1 tablespoon olive oil

4 garlic cloves, finely
sliced

55 g (2¼ oz) butter

125 ml (4 fl oz) single
cream or unsweetened
soya cream

salt and pepper

chopped parsley,
to garnish

RED ONION
GRAVY

1 tablespoon olive oil

1 red onion, sliced

1 tablespoon plain flour

300 ml (½ pint)
vegetable stock

2 tablespoons shoyu
or dark soy sauce

a dash of sugar
(optional)

Real comfort food! Choose your favourite veggie sausages –
Lincolnshire ones are popular in my family – and serve them
with creamy mashed potato and this delicious gravy.

1 First make the gravy. Heat the olive oil in a saucepan
and add the onion. Cook over a gentle heat, covered, for
15 minutes, until lightly browned and caramelized. Stir
from time to time to prevent sticking.

2 Sprinkle the flour into the onion, then pour in the
vegetable stock and bring to the boil, stirring. Add the
shoyu or soy sauce and season with pepper and perhaps
a dash of sugar (you may not need any salt as the soy
sauce is salty). Leave over a very gentle heat.

3 Meanwhile, boil the potatoes in water to cover for
about 20 minutes, or until tender.

4 Once the potatoes are cooking, cook the sausages
according to the packet directions and keep them warm
if necessary.

5 At the same time, heat the olive oil in a small frying pan
over a medium heat and lightly fry the garlic for 1 minute,
until lightly browned.

6 Drain the potatoes, reserving the water, and pass them
through a potato ricer or mash them thoroughly by hand.
Beat in the butter and cream or soya cream to make a
smooth, creamy consistency. Add a small quantity of the
reserved water if needed. Season with salt and pepper.

7 Spoon the mash into a warm serving dish and garnish
with chopped parsley and garlic. Serve the sausages
alongside, topped with the onion gravy.

Refried Beans

SERVES 4

2 tablespoons olive oil

1 large onion, finely
  chopped

2 garlic cloves, chopped

2 × 410 g (13½ oz) cans
  pinto beans, drained

½–1 teaspoon chilli
  powder

salt and pepper

TO SERVE

lettuce leaves

sliced tomatoes

1 large avocado,
  skinned, stoned
  and sliced

soured cream

paprika

chopped coriander

tortilla chips

grated Cheddar cheese
  (optional)

The title of this recipe is derived from the Spanish frijoles refritos,
meaning 'very well cooked' (rather than 'twice cooked'). It's the
accompaniments that really make this lovely dish, so don't hold back.

1 Heat the olive oil in a large, heavy-based saucepan,
add the onion, cover and cook gently for 10 minutes,
stirring from time to time. Stir in the garlic and cook
for 1–2 minutes.

2 Add the pinto beans to the pan, along with the chilli
powder, and salt and pepper. Mash the beans roughly
with a potato masher or wooden spoon so that they cling
together, but keep plenty of texture. Stir well so that they
don't stick to the pan. The beans are ready when they're
piping hot.

3 Arrange lettuce leaves on a large serving plate and
spoon the beans into the centre. Arrange tomato and
avocado slices around the edge, swirl soured cream,
paprika and chopped coriander on top and serve with
tortilla chips and grated Cheddar, if liked.

Meals for Special Occasions

Mushroom and Spinach Filo Parcels

SERVES 4

12 sheets of filo
   pastry, 23 × 23 cm
   (9 × 9 inches) each

4 tablespoons olive oil

pretty salad leaves,
   to serve

WILD
MUSHROOM
AND SPINACH
FILLING

2 × 250 g (8 oz) packets
   spinach

2 tablespoons olive oil

1 red onion, chopped

625 g (1¼ lb) mixed wild
   mushrooms, wiped
   and sliced

4 garlic cloves, crushed

freshly grated nutmeg

25 g (1 oz) butter

salt and pepper

BALSAMIC
DRIZZLE

2 tablespoons balsamic
   vinegar

4 tablespoons olive oil

Packets of filo vary in size: here you need 12 sheets at least 23 cm (9 inches) square. The better the balsamic vinegar, the better the drizzle – thick, sweet and shiny.

1 First make the filling. Put 1 packet of the spinach into a large bowl and cover with a kettleful of boiling water. Leave to stand for 3–4 minutes until wilted, then drain. Repeat with the remaining packet, then set aside.

2 Heat the olive oil in a large saucepan and gently fry the onion for 5 minutes without browning. Add the mushrooms and cook for a further 7–10 minutes, or until they are tender. If they make a lot of liquid, increase the heat and let the water bubble away. Stir in the garlic and cook for a further 2–3 minutes.

3 Season the mushrooms to taste with salt, pepper and grated nutmeg.

4 Using your hands, take small quantities of the wilted spinach and squeeze out all the water. Stir the butter into the squeezed-out spinach, and season well with salt, pepper and grated nutmeg.

5 To make a parcel, put 1 sheet of filo on a board or work surface and brush with olive oil. Put another sheet over it at an angle, brush with oil, and repeat with a third sheet.

6 Put a quarter of the spinach mixture in the middle of the filo sheets, then heap a quarter of the mushrooms on top. Fold up the sides of the filo and scrunch them at the top so they hold together. Brush all over with olive oil. Make 3 more parcels in the same way and place on a lightly oiled baking sheet.

7 Bake the parcels in a pre-heated oven, 200°C (400°F), Gas Mark 6, for 20 minutes, or until they are crisp and lightly browned.

8 While the parcels are baking, make the balsamic drizzle: simply whisk or shake the balsamic vinegar and olive oil together to make a slightly thickened emulsion.

9 Serve the parcels on individual warm plates, with a little of the balsamic mixture drizzled over and around them, and some pretty salad leaves alongside.

Roasted Butternut Squash

SERVES 4

1 butternut squash

olive oil, for brushing

2 onions, chopped

2 tablespoons olive oil

2 tablespoons chopped sage

175 g (6 oz) Stilton or other blue cheese, roughly crumbled

50 g (2 oz) pine nuts

salt and pepper

SHERRY GRAVY

600 ml (1 pint) water

3 teaspoons vegetable bouillon powder

3 tablespoons soy sauce

1½ tablespoons redcurrant jelly

3 teaspoons cornflour

1½ tablespoons orange juice

1½ tablespoons fino sherry

TO GARNISH

sage sprigs, deep-fried until crisp

Serve this with gravy, cranberry sauce, roast potatoes and sprouts for a lovely (and really easy) festive main course.

1 Cut the butternut squash carefully in half lengthways, scoop out the seeds and brush the inside with olive oil. Place the squash halves in a roasting tin and bake in a preheated oven, 200°C (400°F), Gas Mark 6, for about 35 minutes, or until they are tender. Leave to cool.

2 Fry the onions in 2 tablespoons of the olive oil for about 10 minutes, until soft and golden.

3 Using a small knife, cut round inside the flesh of the squash halves to widen the cavity, so that there is not more than 1 cm (½ inch) of flesh round the edges, and scoop out some of the base with a teaspoon.

4 Mix the scooped-out squash flesh with the onions. Add the sage and Stilton or other blue cheese, and season with salt and pepper. Pile the cheese mixture back into the squash halves and set aside until you are ready to bake.

5 Bake in a preheated oven, 200°C (400°F), Gas Mark 6, for 15 minutes, then scatter with the pine nuts and bake for a further 10 minutes, or until the nuts are golden brown.

6 Meanwhile, make the sherry gravy. Put the water, bouillon powder, soy sauce and redcurrant jelly into a saucepan and bring to the boil. Blend the cornflour with the orange juice and fino sherry. Stir a little of the hot liquid into the cornflour mixture and tip this into the saucepan. Stir well, then simmer over a gentle heat until slightly thickened.

7 To serve, place the squash halves on a warm serving dish and top with deep-fried sage. Hand round the sherry gravy.

Spinach Lasagne

SERVES 6

2 tablespoons olive oil

1 large onion, chopped

900 g (1 lb 13 oz) cooked fresh spinach, chopped, or frozen chopped spinach, thawed

625 g (1¼ lb) medium-fat cream cheese

freshly grated nutmeg

2 × 400 g (13 oz) cans chopped tomatoes

2 garlic cloves, crushed

butter, for greasing

225 g (7½ oz) oven-ready lasagne

350 g (11½ oz) mozzarella cheese, drained and thinly sliced

200 g (7 oz) Parmesan-style cheese, grated

salt and pepper

A lovely big tasty dish, great for a party. The only accompaniment it needs, if any, is a bowl of crisp green salad.

1 Heat the olive oil in a large saucepan, add the onion and fry gently for 10 minutes, until soft but not browned.

2 Remove from the heat and add the spinach and the soft cheese. Season with salt, plenty of pepper and grated nutmeg.

3 Put the tomatoes into a saucepan with the garlic, bring to the boil and simmer for 10 minutes, to make a sauce. Season with salt and pepper.

4 Grease a large, shallow, ovenproof dish with butter and cover the base with one-third of the tomato sauce. Layer one-third of the lasagne on top, followed by one-third each of the spinach mixture, mozzarella and Parmesan-style cheese.

5 Continue like this until all the ingredients are used up, ending with a layer of grated Parmesan-style cheese.

6 Bake in a preheated oven, 200°C (400°F), Gas Mark 6, for about 35 minutes, or until golden brown. Serve hot.

Crisp Tofu with Spicy Sambal

SERVES 4

400 g (13 oz) packet tofu, drained and cut into cubes

plain flour, for dusting

rapeseed oil, for deep-frying

2 tablespoons crushed peanuts, to garnish

SPICY SAMBAL

1 tablespoon olive oil

1 lemon grass stalk, trimmed and finely chopped

1 red chilli, sliced (deseeded if you like)

1 garlic clove, crushed

1 tablespoon soft brown or palm sugar

4 tomatoes, roughly chopped

a small handful of coriander, chopped

2 tablespoons ketjap manis or soy sauce

1 tablespoon prepared tamarind (from a jar)

4 tablespoons water

A favourite tofu dish with its beautiful colour and contrasting flavours and textures. You can get all the ingredients at any large supermarket and they keep well.

1 First make the sambal. Heat the olive oil in a saucepan and fry the lemon grass, chilli and garlic for 1 minute. Remove from the heat and add all the remaining ingredients.

2 Toss the tofu cubes in the flour. Pour enough rapeseed oil into a wok or saucepan to cover the tofu and heat to 180–190°C (356–374°F), or until a cube of bread browns in 30 seconds.

3 Add the tofu and fry until crisp and golden – this may take as long as 10 minutes – making sure it gets nice and crisp (fry in 2 batches if necessary). Drain on kitchen paper.

4 Serve the tofu with the sambal spooned over, sprinkled with the crushed peanuts.

White Nut Roast with Herb Stuffing

My family's Christmas favourite. I've made various versions over the years; this one is particularly light and delicious. Serve with Red Onion Gravy (see page 73).

SERVES 8–10

50 g (2 oz) butter, plus extra for greasing

3–4 tablespoons dried breadcrumbs, for coating

1 large onion, chopped

1 teaspoon dried thyme

1 tablespoon plain flour

300 ml (½ pint) milk or soya milk

225 g (7½ oz) mixed white nuts, finely ground: use cashew nuts, blanched almonds and pine nuts

100 g (3½ oz) fresh white breadcrumbs

freshly grated nutmeg

2 egg whites

salt and pepper

HERB STUFFING

175 g (6 oz) fresh white breadcrumbs

100 g (4 oz) butter

4 tablespoons chopped parsley

grated rind of ½ lemon

2 tablespoons grated onion

1 teaspoon each dried marjoram and thyme

2 egg yolks

1 Grease a 900 g (1 lb 13 oz) loaf tin with butter and line with a strip of buttered greaseproof paper to cover the base of the tin and extend up the narrow sides. Sprinkle with the dried breadcrumbs.

2 Heat the 50 g (2 oz) butter in a saucepan, add the onion and fry gently for 10 minutes, until soft, without browning. Add the thyme and flour and cook for 1–2 minutes, then add the milk and stir until thickened. Remove from the heat and add the nuts and fresh white breadcrumbs. Season generously with salt, pepper and grated nutmeg.

3 Whisk the egg whites until they are stiff but not dry, then fold them into the nut mixture.

4 To make the herb stuffing, thoroughly mix all the ingredients together and season with salt and pepper.

5 Spoon half the nut mixture into the tin in an even layer. With your hands, form the stuffing into a flat layer that will fit over the top of the nut mixture; put it into the tin on top of the nut mixture. Cover the stuffing with the remaining nut mixture.

6 Level the top, cover with buttered foil and bake in a preheated oven, 190°C (375°F), Gas Mark 5, for 1 hour, or until the loaf is firm in the centre. Remove the foil for the last 15 minutes of cooking time to allow the top to brown.

7 Let the loaf stand for 4–5 minutes, then slip a knife around the edges and invert it on a warm serving dish.

MEALS FOR SPECIAL OCCASIONS

Red Onion and Goats' Cheese Tart

SERVES 4–6

150 g (5 oz) **salted butter**

175 g (6 oz) **spelt flour, sifted**

2–4 **tablespoons cold water**

RED ONION AND GOATS' CHEESE FILLING

1 tablespoon **olive oil**

500 g (1 lb) **red onions, thinly sliced**

1 tablespoon **golden caster sugar**

1½ **tablespoons fino sherry or red wine**

1 tablespoon **red wine vinegar**

3 × 100 g (3½ oz) **goats' cheeses with soft rinds**

salt and pepper

The pastry for this tart needs no kneading, rolling or 'resting'. I make it with spelt flour, which gives it a sweet, melt-in-the-mouth quality.

1 Start with the filling. Heat the oil in a large saucepan, add the onions and cook, covered, for about 15 minutes, until they're very tender, stirring every 5 minutes.

2 Add the sugar, fino sherry or red wine, and the wine vinegar. Let the mixture simmer gently, without a lid, for about 30 minutes, until it is thick and sticky and there's hardly any liquid left. Remove from the heat, season with salt and pepper, and leave to cool.

3 Meanwhile, make the pastry. Rub the butter into the flour with your fingertips, or use a food processor, until the mixture looks like breadcrumbs. Add 2 tablespoons of the water and mix to a dough, adding more water if necessary.

4 Gather the pastry into a ball, then press it straight into a 23-cm (9-inch) tart tin. Press it right out to the edges and up the sides, covering the tart tin thinly.

5 Prick the base of the pastry all over, and place a sheet of nonstick paper on top, with a few crusts of bread or some dried beans on top of that to weigh it down.

6 Bake in a preheated oven, 200°C (400°F), Gas Mark 6, for 10 minutes, then remove the paper and the bread or beans and return the tart to the oven for another 10 minutes, until the pastry is set and a light golden colour.

7 Spread the onion mixture over the tart base. Crumble the goats' cheeses over the onions, to cover them. Return the tart to the oven and cook for 20 minutes, until the cheese has melted and browned.

Croustade of Asparagus Hollandaise

SERVES 6

1 kg (2 lb) asparagus tips (thin if possible), trimmed

CROUSTADE

150 g (5 oz) fresh white breadcrumbs

150 g (5 oz) cashew nuts, finely ground in a coffee grinder (or use ground almonds)

150 g (5 oz) butter

3 garlic cloves, finely chopped

75 g (3 oz) onion, finely grated

150 g (5 oz) pine nuts

5 teaspoons water

HOLLANDAISE SAUCE

250 g (8 oz) butter, cut into chunks

4 egg yolks

2 tablespoons lemon juice

salt and pepper

This crisp, nutty base topped with asparagus in luxurious hollandaise sauce is indisputably classic as it's a variation on one of my very earliest and most popular recipes.

1 First make the croustade. Mix together the breadcrumbs, ground nuts, butter, garlic and onion, by hand or by whizzing in a food processor, then stir in the pine nuts and water and mix to make a dough.

2 Press the mixture down lightly into the base of a 30-cm (12-inch) shallow ovenproof dish or pizza dish. Bake in a preheated oven, 200°C (400°F), Gas Mark 6, for 15–20 minutes, until crisp and golden brown. Set aside.

3 Cook the asparagus in boiling water for 3–4 minutes, or until tender, then drain.

4 Meanwhile, make the hollandaise sauce. Melt the butter gently in a saucepan without browning it. Put the egg yolks, lemon juice and some salt and pepper into a liquidizer or food processor and whiz for 1 minute, until the mixture is thick. With the motor running, pour in the melted butter in a thin, steady stream – the sauce will thicken. Let it stand for 1–2 minutes.

5 Pile the asparagus on top of the croustade, pour the sauce over and serve at once.

Artichoke Heart and Basil Frittata

SERVES 4

2 × 290 g (9½ oz) jars chargrilled, halved artichoke hearts in oil

225 g (7½ oz) Gruyère or Emmental cheese, grated

8 eggs, beaten

a handful of basil, roughly chopped

salt and pepper

With chargrilled artichokes in the cupboard, cheese and eggs in the fridge, and this recipe you'll never be short of a great emergency meal.

1 Drain the artichoke hearts but save the oil. Heat 2 tablespoons of the oil in a 28-cm (11-inch) frying pan.

2 Arrange the artichoke hearts in a single layer on the bottom of the pan, sprinkle with half the Gruyère or Emmental, then pour the eggs evenly over the top. Season with salt and pepper and top with the basil and remaining cheese.

3 Set the pan over a moderate heat, cover with a lid or plate and cook for about 5 minutes, or until the base is set and getting browned. Meanwhile, preheat the grill to high.

4 Remove the covering from the pan and put the pan under the grill for about 10 minutes, or until the frittata has puffed up and browned, and is set in the centre. Serve straightaway.

Whole Baked Brie in Filo

SERVES 6

2 × 275 g (9 oz) packets
  filo pastry

50–75 ml (2–3 fl oz)
  olive oil

1 whole Brie cheese,
  20–25 cm (8–10 inches)
  in diameter, firm and
  under-ripe if possible

steamed green beans,
  to serve

APRICOT SAUCE

500 g (1 lb) jar apricot
  conserve

4 tablespoons lemon
  juice

*The combination of crisp pastry and hot, melting cheese is always
irresistible and the sweet apricot sauce balances the richness perfectly.
A wonderful party dish.*

1 Place 1 sheet of filo pastry on a large baking sheet and
brush with a little olive oil. Place another sheet so that it
overlaps it, and brush with more oil. Repeat until you have
used all the sheets in 1 of the packets. The idea is to make
a square of layers of filo that is big enough to form a base
for the Brie and that can also be brought up the sides. It's
better to have too large a square than too small because
you will be trimming off excess pastry later.

2 Put the Brie on top of the filo, then cut the filo, allowing
10 cm (4 inches) all round the Brie. Now, use the filo sheets
in the second packet to build up more layers on top of
the Brie – these need to cover the cheese with about 5 cm
(2 inches) to spare around the sides. Fold up the bottom
layer of filo to meet the top layer and roll them together
to secure them and form a decorative seal around the Brie.
Brush with more oil and make a steam hole in the middle.

3 Place the filo parcel, on its baking sheet, in a preheated
oven, 200°C (400°F), Gas Mark 6, and bake for 30–40
minutes, until the pastry is golden brown and crisp.
Remove from the oven and leave to stand for 10–15
minutes, then slide the pie carefully on to a large platter.
Once cut, the Brie will ooze all over the place, so make
sure it's on a big enough platter, preferably with sides.

4 To make the apricot sauce, put the apricot conserve
and the lemon juice into a small saucepan and bring to
the boil. Pour into a jug and serve along with the Brie
parcel, accompanied by steamed green beans.

Creamy Cashew Korma

SERVES 4

- 1 tablespoon rapeseed oil
- 1 large onion, finely chopped
- 2 garlic cloves, crushed
- 1 teaspoon turmeric
- 1 tablespoon ground cumin
- 1 tablespoon ground coriander
- 50 g (2 oz) cashew nuts
- 400 ml (14 fl oz) can coconut milk
- 400 ml (14 fl oz) water
- a small handful of fresh curry leaves (optional)
- 175 g (6 oz) okra, topped and tailed
- 250 g (8 oz) cauliflower florets
- 250 g (8 oz) broccoli florets
- salt and pepper
- chopped fresh coriander, to garnish
- cooked white Basmati rice, to serve

The cashew nuts thicken and enrich the sauce in this fragrantly spiced dish. Perfect accompanied by white Basmati rice.

1 Heat the rapeseed oil in a large saucepan and add the onion. Cover and cook gently for about 10 minutes, until tender, without browning. Stir in the garlic, turmeric, ground cumin and ground coriander, and cook for another 1–2 minutes.

2 Grind the cashew nuts to a powder in a coffee grinder or food processor, or use the fine grater in a hand mill. Add the nuts to the pan, along with the coconut milk.

3 For a really smooth sauce, you can purée the whole lot in a liquidizer or food processor (or use a stick blender in the saucepan) or, if you prefer some texture, leave it as it is.

4 Return the mixture to the pan, if you've puréed it, and add the water and the curry leaves, if using. Leave to simmer for 20–30 minutes, stirring from time to time, until the korma has thickened.

5 Just before the sauce is ready, put the okra, cauliflower and broccoli into a pan containing a depth of 5 cm (2 inches) of boiling water. Cover and cook for about 6 minutes, or until the tender. Drain, and add the vegetables to the sauce, stirring gently. Season with salt and pepper.

6 You can serve the korma at once, but if there's time let it rest for a while – even overnight – for the flavours to intensify. Then gently reheat. Scatter with chopped fresh coriander, and serve with white Basmati rice.

Pea, Spinach and Mint Pithiviers

SERVES 4

250 g (8 oz) baby
   spinach leaves

200 g (7 oz) frozen petits
   pois, thawed

4 tablespoons chopped
   mint

375 g (12 oz) frozen
   ready-rolled all-butter
   puff pastry

200 g (7 oz) Boursin
   garlic and herb cream
   cheese

4 tablespoons cream,
   to glaze

salt and pepper

I love the balance of flavours in these flaky golden pies, and the way the creamy filling oozes out when you cut into them. Perfect for a special occasion.

1 Cook the spinach in a dry saucepan for 1–2 minutes until wilted, then drain and cool. Season with salt and pepper. Mash the peas with the mint – give them a quick whiz in a food processor or with a stick blender – so they hold together a bit.

2 Lay the puff pastry on a board and roll it out to make it even thinner, then cut it into 4 × 10-cm (4-inch) circles for the bases, and 4 slightly larger ones, about 17 cm (6¾ inches) – it's useful to cut round a saucer – to go over the top.

3 Place the smaller circles on a baking sheet. Put a layer of spinach on top of each circle, leaving about 1 cm (½ inch) free round the edges. Put a quarter of the Boursin on top of the spinach, then heap the peas on top and around the Boursin. Cover with the larger pastry circles, pressing the edges neatly together and crimping with your fingers or the prongs of a fork. Make a steam hole in the centre of each and decorate the top with little cuts spiralling out from the centre, like a traditional pithivier, if you wish. All this can be done in advance. When you are ready to cook, brush the tops with the cream.

4 Bake the pithiviers in a preheated oven, 200°C (400°F), Gas Mark 6, for about 25 minutes, or until they are puffed up, golden brown and crisp. Serve at once.

Green Risotto

SERVES 4

1 tablespoon olive oil

1 onion, chopped

1 celery stick, finely chopped

125 g (4 oz) runner beans, trimmed and cut into 2.5-cm (1-inch) lengths

1 teaspoon vegetable bouillon powder

1 garlic clove, crushed

400 g (13 oz) carnaroli or risotto rice

250 ml (8 fl oz) white wine

125 g (4 oz) baby leaf spinach

125 g (4 oz) fresh or frozen petits pois

3–4 tablespoons chopped herbs – parsley, mint, dill, chives; whatever is available

salt and pepper

grated or shaved Parmesan-style cheese, to serve (optional)

It's hard to believe that such a delectable risotto is actually low in fat; roasted tomatoes complement it perfectly.

1 Heat the olive oil in a large saucepan. Add the onion and celery, stir, then cover and cook gently for 7 minutes without browning.

2 Meanwhile, cook the runner beans in boiling water to cover for 4–5 minutes, or until just tender. Drain and set aside, reserving the liquid. Make the liquid up to 1.2 litres (2 pints) and put into a pan with the bouillon powder. Bring to the boil and keep warm.

3 Add the garlic and rice to the onion and celery in the pan and stir well. Add half the white wine and continue cooking, stirring all the time, until the wine has bubbled away. Repeat the process with the remaining wine, then add the hot stock in the same way, a ladleful at a time.

4 When the rice is tender and all or most of the stock has been used up – about 25 minutes – add the spinach, reserved beans, petits pois and herbs, cover and leave to stand for 5 minutes, until the spinach is cooked.

5 Season with salt and pepper, and serve at once with a little Parmesan-style cheese, if liked.

Cheese Fondue

SERVES 4

1 garlic clove, halved

1 white French stick, cut into bite-sized cubes

1 wholemeal French stick, cut into bite-sized cubes

300 ml (½ pint) dry white wine or cider

400 g (13 oz) Gruyère or Edam cheese, grated

1 tablespoon cornflour

2 tablespoons kirsch or gin (optional)

2 teaspoons lemon juice

freshly grated nutmeg

salt and pepper

If you can't find vegetarian Gruyère (and it's elusive), Edam makes an excellent substitute. Try it: you won't be disappointed.

1 Rub the garlic halves around the inside of a medium-sized saucepan, then discard them. Place the French stick cubes in a preheated oven, 180°C (350°F), Gas Mark 4, to warm.

2 Put all but 4 tablespoons of the wine or cider into the saucepan and bring just to the boil, then add the Gruyère or Edam and stir over a gentle heat until melted.

3 Mix the cornflour with the remaining wine or cider and the kirsch or gin, if using. Pour this into the cheese mixture, stirring until slightly thickened.

4 Remove the cheese mixture from the heat and add the lemon juice. Season to taste with salt, pepper and grated nutmeg. Put the warmed bread cubes into 2 baskets, mixing up white and wholemeal.

5 Place the pan of fondue in the centre of the dining table. Use long forks to spear the bread cubes and dip them into the cheese fondue.

Roasted Marinated Tofu with Pak Choi

SERVES 4

400 g (13 oz) packet tofu, drained

4 tablespoons shoyu or dark soy sauce

2 tablespoons toasted sesame oil

2 tablespoons water

2 tablespoons lemon juice

5-cm (2-inch) piece of fresh root ginger, finely grated

2 garlic cloves, crushed

MUSHROOMS AND PAK CHOI

200 g (7 oz) baby button mushrooms

1 tablespoon olive oil

4–6 pak choi (2 packets), washed and halved from top to root

salt and pepper

SATAY SAUCE

2 tablespoons peanut butter

3 tablespoons coconut milk

1 teaspoon shoyu or dark soy sauce

TO GARNISH

2–3 tablespoons salted peanuts, crushed

2–4 tablespoons chopped coriander

There are several parts to this dish, but they're all quick and easy. Precooking the tofu makes it really soak up the marinade: it's so tasty!

1 Blot the tofu dry on kitchen paper and cut into thin strips about 5 mm (¼ inch) thick: you will get about 12 from the block.

2 Cook the tofu strips in a dry frying pan over a gentle heat for about 10 minutes, until they are dry and golden on one side, then turn them over and cook the second side in the same way. The tofu needs to be dry and firm.

3 In a large, shallow dish that's big enough to hold all the tofu slices in a single layer, mix the shoyu, sesame oil, water, lemon juice, ginger and garlic. Put the cooked tofu strips on top, turn them in the marinade, and leave to marinate for at least 1 hour.

4 To make the satay sauce, just mix all the ingredients together. Set aside. (You can freeze leftover coconut milk.)

5 Just before serving the meal, heat the tofu under a moderate grill for about 10 minutes, until heated through.

6 Fry the mushrooms in the olive oil for 4–5 minutes, until tender. Keep these warm.

7 Cook the pak choi. Bring 1 cm (½ inch) of water to the boil in a large saucepan, put in the pak choi and cover the pan. Cook for about 4 minutes, or until the pak choi is just tender. Drain well and season with salt and pepper.

8 Divide the pak choi, mushrooms and tofu between 4 warm plates, heaping them up attractively. Drizzle the satay sauce over and around, scatter with crushed peanuts and chopped coriander, and serve.

Mushroom Pâté en Croûte

SERVES 6

450 g (14½ oz) frozen
  puff pastry made
  with butter, thawed

egg yolk, for brushing

MUSHROOM
PÂTÉ

25 g (1 oz) butter

1 onion, chopped

900 g (1 lb 13 oz)
  mushrooms, washed
  and finely chopped

2 garlic cloves, crushed

2 tablespoons chopped
  parsley

100 g (3½ oz) dried
  wholemeal
  breadcrumbs

2 tablespoons lemon
  juice

salt and pepper

With its flaky golden pastry coating, this makes a splendid centrepiece dish for a special occasion or celebration; everyone loves it.

1 First make the mushroom pâté. Heat the butter in a large saucepan, add the onion and fry gently, without browning, for 10 minutes. Add the mushrooms and fry for 20–30 minutes, until all the liquid has evaporated.

2 Remove from the heat and add the garlic, parsley, breadcrumbs, lemon juice and some salt and pepper. Leave the mixture to cool.

3 Roll one-third of the pastry into a rectangle measuring 15 × 30 cm (6 × 12 inches). Place on a baking sheet and spoon the mushroom mixture on top, heaping it up well. Brush the edges of the pastry with water.

4 Roll out the remaining pastry to a rectangle measuring 23 × 30 cm (9 × 12 inches).

5 Fold the rectangle in half lengthways and make diagonal cuts with scissors to give a fancy finish, if you like. Open out and carefully place over the mushroom mixture; be careful to maintain the shape of the mushroom mixture.

6 Press the pastry edges together and trim. If you haven't already made diagonal cuts in the top, make a few steam holes and brush with egg yolk. Bake in a preheated oven, 220°C (425°F), Gas Mark 7, for 30 minutes, until golden brown. Serve hot or cold.

Salads, Vegetables and Accompaniments

Quinoa and Red Grape Salad

SERVES 4

175 g (6 oz) quinoa

450 ml (¾ pint) water

2 tablespoons flaked
  almonds

250 g (8 oz) seedless red
  grapes, halved

3–4 spring onions,
  chopped

4 teaspoons clear honey

4 teaspoons cider
  vinegar

salt and pepper

little gem lettuce leaves
  and watercress,
  to serve

Quinoa is a lovely grain and very nourishing. The sweetness of the grapes and honey balances its slight bitterness perfectly, and the almonds add crunch.

1 Put the quinoa into a saucepan with the water. Bring to the boil, then cover and cook gently for 15 minutes, until the quinoa is tender. Remove from the heat and leave to stand, covered, for a few more minutes, or until cold.

2 Spread the almonds out in a grill pan or shallow roasting tin that will fit under the grill. Put under a preheated hot grill for a minute or so until they turn golden. Give them a stir if necessary so they cook evenly, but watch them like a hawk as they burn very easily. As soon as they're done, remove them from the grill and transfer to a plate, to ensure they don't go on cooking in the residual heat.

3 Put the quinoa into a bowl with the grapes, spring onions, honey, cider vinegar and some salt and pepper and mix gently. This can be done in advance if you like.

4 Just before serving, stir in the flaked almonds. It's especially nice if they're still slightly warm from the grill. Serve with crunchy little gem lettuce leaves, perhaps mixed with some watercress.

Pecan and Pomegranate Salad

SERVES 4

100 g (3½ oz) pecan nuts, roughly broken

1 tablespoon balsamic vinegar

2 tablespoons olive oil

250 g (8 oz) peppery leaves, such as rocket or watercress

1 pomegranate

salt and pepper

A gorgeous mix of colours, flavours and textures: crunchy pecans, peppery leaves and juicy sweet-sour pomegranate jewels... Great with Twice-baked Individual Soufflés (see page 24), or just some fluffy couscous.

1 Spread the pecan nuts out on a baking sheet and place in a preheated oven, 180°C (350°F), Gas Mark 4, for about 12 minutes, or until they are lightly browned and aromatic. Remove from the oven and tip on to a plate to prevent them from burning.

2 Mix the balsamic vinegar, olive oil and some salt and pepper in a large salad bowl to make a dressing.

3 Put the leaves on top of the dressing, but don't toss them. Halve the pomegranate as you would a grapefruit and turn the skin inside out to make the seeds pop out. Add the seeds to the leaves, along with the pecans.

4 Toss the salad and serve immediately.

Super Caesar Salad

SERVES 4

1 large or romaine lettuce, washed and torn into bite-sized pieces

a handful of caper berries, drained and rinsed

60 g (2¼ oz) packet roasted and salted macadamia nuts

DRESSING

4 tablespoons mayonnaise

1 tablespoon lemon juice

Tabasco sauce

6 tablespoons flaked Parmesan-style cheese

pepper

Of course vegetarians don't eat fish, so instead of anchovies this Caesar is spiced up with Tabasco sauce and caper berries with macadamia nuts for crunch.

1 First make the dressing. Mix the mayonnaise, lemon juice and enough Tabasco to give a good zing. Stir in half the Parmesan-style cheese. Grind in some pepper; you won't need extra salt because of the caper berries, macadamia nuts and cheese.

2 At the last minute, just before you want to serve the salad, put the lettuce into a salad bowl and add most of the caper berries, half the nuts and the dressing.

3 Toss the salad, then top with the remaining caper berries, nuts and cheese, and serve immediately.

Mango and Watercress Salad

SERVES 4

1 large ripe mango

1 small red onion, finely chopped

½ small bunch of coriander, roughly chopped

grated rind of 2 limes

juice of 1 lime

1 green or red serrano chilli, deseeded and finely chopped (optional)

salt and pepper

80 g (3¼ oz) packet or bunch of watercress, washed and trimmed as necessary, to serve

This unusual salad is refreshing and delicious with spicy vegetable and rice dishes and is very easy to make.

1 Hold the mango over a chopping board, stalk end uppermost, and make 2 sharp cuts, each about 5 mm (¼ inch) from the stalk, from top to bottom. You will feel the large flat stone against the knife as you cut. The 2 halves will fall away.

2 Cut away the peel from the mango halves, then cut the flesh into small pieces and put them into a bowl.

3 Add the onion, coriander and lime rind and juice, and enough of the chilli to give the kind of kick you like. Mix gently and season with enough salt and pepper to balance the sweetness of the mango. The salad will keep – and improve – for an hour or so.

4 At the last minute, arrange the watercress on a flat serving dish and spoon the mango salad on top, leaving a border of watercress round the edges. Serve at once.

Middle Eastern Salad Platter

SERVES 4

1 bunch of spring
onions, lightly
trimmed

1 bunch of radishes,
washed, leaves still
attached

1 small bunch of mint

1 small bunch of flat
leaf parsley

2 green peppers,
deseeded and cut into
wedges

4 tomatoes, quartered

125 g (4 oz) chillies
preserved in brine,
rinsed and drained

125 g (4 oz) olives, such
as kalamata, or green
olives if you prefer

GRATED CARROT

4 carrots, grated

juice of 1 orange

chopped chives,
to garnish

TZATZIKI

½ cucumber, peeled
and diced

½ small onion, finely
chopped

150 ml (¼ pint) thick
Greek yogurt

3 mint sprigs, chopped

salt and pepper

*This is fresh, easy and colourful; perfect for serving as a starter,
or with bean or rice dishes, for a complete summery lunch.*

1 You can prepare the grated carrot and tzatziki in
advance, then assemble the salad at the last minute so
that all the herbs and vegetables are cool and bursting
with freshness.

2 Mix the grated carrots with the orange juice; this
provides a sweet dressing and preserves the bright colour.
It will keep in a covered container in the fridge for at least
24 hours.

3 For the tzatziki, put the diced cucumber and chopped
onion into a sieve, mix with a good sprinkling of salt and
leave for about 30 minutes, to draw out excess moisture.
Pat dry with kitchen paper, then mix the cucumber and
onion with the yogurt, chopped mint, a little more salt if
necessary and pepper to taste. Chill until ready to serve.

4 To assemble the salad, put the grated carrot and tzatziki
into small serving bowls and scatter chopped chives over
the carrot. Arrange the bowls, spring onions, radishes,
mint, parsley, peppers, tomatoes, chillies and olives on
a large serving platter or tray.

Butter Bean Salad

SERVES 4

2 × 420 g (14 oz) cans butter beans, drained and rinsed

¼–½ teaspoon dried red chilli flakes

2 teaspoons maple syrup

2 tablespoons rice vinegar

2 teaspoons toasted sesame oil

2 teaspoons shoyu or tamari

2 spring onions, thinly sliced

3–4 tablespoons roughly chopped celery leaves

50 g (2 oz) salted peanuts, crushed

pepper

Lift sensible butter beans to another level with this mixture of sweet and sour, salty and spicy. The glossy dressing coats the mealy beans and peanuts give a contrasting crunch.

1 Put the butter beans into a bowl, add the red chilli flakes, maple syrup, rice vinegar, sesame oil, shoyu or tamari and a grinding of pepper and stir gently to mix.

2 Add the spring onions and celery leaves, then stir again. Add the crushed peanuts just before serving, so that they remain crisp.

Ratatouille

SERVES 4

3 tablespoons olive oil

2 large onions, chopped

3 large red peppers,
  deseeded and sliced

3 garlic cloves, crushed

450 g (14½ oz)
  courgettes, cut into
  even-sized pieces

450 g (14½ oz)
  aubergines, diced

700 g (1 lb 7 oz)
  tomatoes, skinned
  and chopped

salt and pepper

chopped parsley,
  to garnish

*I love this summery dish served either on its own with some rice,
or accompanying a main course. It's also excellent cold.*

1 Heat the olive oil in a large saucepan and fry the onions
and peppers gently for 5 minutes.

2 Add the garlic, courgettes and aubergines. Stir gently,
then cover and cook over a low heat for about 25 minutes,
until all the vegetables are tender.

3 Add the tomatoes, stir gently and cook, uncovered, for
about 5 minutes, to heat through. Season with some salt
and pepper and sprinkle with chopped parsley. Serve hot
or cold.

Courgette Ribbons

SERVES 4

500 g (1 lb) courgettes (about 3 medium-sized ones)

juice of ½ lemon or lime

1 tablespoon olive oil or toasted sesame oil

2 tablespoons chopped flat leaf parsley or coriander

½–1 teaspoon coarsely crushed black peppercorns or sesame seeds

salt

You can vary the type of oil, herbs and seasoning to complement the meal: olive oil, parsley and black pepper for Mediterranean food, sesame oil, coriander and sesame seeds for Asian.

1 Trim the courgettes, then use a potato peeler or a mandolin to cut them into long, thin ribbons.

2 Just before you want to serve the courgettes, put them into a sieve or colander set over a deep bowl. Pour a kettleful of boiling water over them and leave for 2–3 minutes, then drain.

3 Tip the water out of the bowl and put in the drained courgette ribbons along with the lemon or lime juice, olive or sesame oil, parsley or coriander, peppercorns or sesame seeds, and salt to taste.

4 Serve at once, though this is also good warm or cold.

Roasted Asparagus with Wasabi

SERVES 4

500 g (1 lb) asparagus, trimmed

2 tablespoons toasted sesame oil

salt and pepper

WASABI
VINAIGRETTE

1 packet (2 teaspoons) wasabi powder

2 tablespoons warm water

1 tablespoon rice vinegar

1 tablespoon flavourless vegetable oil, such as grapeseed

2 tablespoons toasted sesame oil

Roasting is my favourite way to cook asparagus – it's so easy and really concentrates the flavour – and the Japanese flavourings supply the surprise element that makes this special.

1 Toss the asparagus in the sesame oil, spread out on a baking sheet and sprinkle with salt. Roast in a preheated oven, 220°C (425°F), Gas Mark 7, for about 15 minutes, or until just tender and lightly browned in places.

2 To make the wasabi vinaigrette, put the wasabi into a lidded jar, add the warm water and mix to a paste. Add the rice vinegar, vegetable oil, sesame oil and some salt and pepper, put the lid on and shake vigorously for a few seconds until smooth.

3 Arrange the asparagus on individual plates and drizzle the vinaigrette on top. Serve hot, warm or cold.

Braised Baby Carrots and Fennel

SERVES 4

2 bunches (about 750 g/
 1½ lb) of baby carrots

400 g (13 oz) baby fennel

4 tablespoons olive oil

4 garlic cloves, sliced

300 ml (½ pint) water

1–2 tablespoons lemon
 juice

salt and pepper

chopped parsley,
 to garnish

A lovely relaxed dish for entertaining, or any time you want an easy vegetable accompaniment that looks and tastes beautiful.

1 If the carrots are really young, just scrub them; if they're older, peel them, but in either case keep them whole and leave 1 cm (½ inch) or so of the green stems attached at the top. If the fennel is really young and tender, just trim the tops; if it's older, trim the base and peel off any damaged outer layers and discard these.

2 Put the carrots and fennel into a saucepan with the olive oil, garlic, water, lemon juice and some salt and pepper and bring to the boil. Reduce the heat, cover the pan and cook gently for about 30 minutes, checking occasionally to make sure the vegetables are not sticking. They're done when they feel very tender to the point of a knife, and the water has reduced to a syrupy golden glaze.

3 Transfer the vegetables to a warm serving dish and scatter with chopped parsley.

Crisp Roasted Parsnips with Sage

SERVES 4

700 g (1 lb 7 oz) parsnips, scrubbed

2 tablespoons plain flour

4 tablespoons olive oil

leaves from 2–3 sage sprigs

sea salt

The secret with these is to get them really tender before you start roasting them; that way they come out crisp on the outside and tender within.

1 Cut the parsnips into chunky pieces.

2 Put the parsnips into a saucepan with cold water to cover and bring to the boil. Cover and simmer until they feel very tender to the point of a sharp knife. Drain well, then toss gently in the flour.

3 Pour the olive oil into a roasting tin and place in a preheated oven, 200°C (400°F), Gas Mark 6, for 4–5 minutes to heat up.

4 Tip the parsnips into the tin and turn them gently to coat them all over with the oil.

5 Roast for about 35 minutes, or until the parsnips are crisp and crunchy all over, turning them once or twice during the cooking. Stir in the sage leaves about 10 minutes before the parsnips are done, so that they get crunchy too.

6 Sprinkle with a little sea salt and serve.

Aubergine Schnitzel

SERVES 4

2 aubergines

olive oil, for frying

salad leaves and lemon
  wedges, to serve

MARINADE

2 tablespoons lemon
  juice

2 tablespoons ume
  plum seasoning or red
  wine vinegar

2 tablespoons olive oil

a few drops of Tabasco
  sauce

salt and pepper

COATING

4 tablespoons cornflour

4–5 tablespoons water

140 g (4½ oz) packet
  dried breadcrumbs

TARTARE
SAUCE

6 tablespoons
  mayonnaise

2 tablespoons small
  capers, rinsed

2 tablespoons small
  gherkins, drained and
  chopped

2 teaspoons finely
  chopped onion

2 tablespoons finely
  chopped flat leaf
  parsley

a few drops of Tabasco
  sauce

*A leafy green salad complements these crisp aubergine slices; or make
a more substantial meal with steamed green beans and creamy mash.*

1 Cut the stalks off the aubergines and remove the peel.
Cut lengthways into 2-cm (¾-inch) slices. You need 4 good
slices. Save the less perfect slices to use in another recipe.

2 Score the slices on both sides with criss-cross cuts
without going right through to the other side.

3 In a large, shallow dish, make the marinade by mixing
the lemon juice, ume plum seasoning or wine vinegar,
olive oil, a few drops of Tabasco and salt and pepper.

4 Lay the aubergine slices in the marinade. Leave them
for 1 hour, turning them so that both sides get covered.

5 Make the tartare sauce: mix everything together.
Put into a small serving bowl and set aside.

6 To coat the aubergine slices, mix the cornflour with
4 tablespoons of the water, then add enough of the
remaining water just to loosen the mixture but not make
it sloppy: it needs to remain sticky. Dip the aubergine
slices in the cornflour mixture.

7 Heat 5 mm (¼ inch) olive oil in a frying pan. Fry the
aubergine slices gently – you will probably have to do them
in at least 2 batches – first on one side and then on the
other, until they are tender. This will take up to 10 minutes.

8 Blot the aubergine on kitchen paper. Keep uncovered
in a warm oven while you cook the remaining schnitzels.

9 Serve the schnitzels with the tartare sauce, salad leaves
and lemon wedges.

Roast Potatoes with Balsamic Vinegar

SERVES 4

1 kg (2 lb) potatoes, peeled and cut into 1-cm (½-inch) chunks

rapeseed oil, for roasting

sea salt

balsamic vinegar

Everyone loves crisp roast potatoes, and the salt and balsamic seasoning make these irresistible!

1 Put the potatoes into a saucepan, cover with water and bring to the boil, then reduce the heat and simmer for 7 minutes.

2 Pour 5 mm (¼ inch) of oil into a roasting tin large enough to hold the potatoes in a single layer, and place in a preheated oven, 200°C (400°F), Gas Mark 6, until smoking hot.

3 Drain the potatoes and put them back into the saucepan, then put the lid on the pan and shake to roughen the outsides and make them roast more crisply.

4 Tip the potatoes into the hot oil and turn them with a large spoon so that the oil covers them all over. Roast for about 35 minutes, or until the potatoes are golden and crisp, turning them over when the undersides are done.

5 Using a draining spoon, transfer the potatoes to a warm serving dish. Sprinkle generously with sea salt, drizzle with balsamic vinegar and serve.

Gratin Dauphinois

SERVES 6

40 g (1½ oz) butter

700 g (1 lb 7 oz) potatoes, peeled and sliced as thinly as possible

freshly grated nutmeg (optional)

1 large garlic clove, crushed

150 ml (¼ pint) double cream

150 ml (¼ pint) water

salt and pepper

This brings a luxury touch to any meal, though I think it's best of all eaten on its own – in which case this quantity will serve 2–3 people. Pure indulgence!

1 Use half of the butter to grease a shallow ovenproof dish generously.

2 Put the potato slices into a colander and rinse well under the cold tap; drain and dry on kitchen paper.

3 Layer the potato slices in the prepared dish, seasoning with salt and pepper, and nutmeg if using. Put a smear of crushed garlic between each layer.

4 Mix the cream and water, then pour evenly over the top of the potatoes and dot with the remaining butter.

5 Bake in a preheated oven, 160°C (325°F), Gas Mark 3, uncovered, for 1½–2 hours, until the potatoes feel tender when pierced with the point of a knife. Serve hot.

Jamaican Jerk Sweet Potato

SERVES 4

4 sweet potatoes, about 350 g (11½ oz) each

lime wedges and soft bread, to serve (optional)

JERK SPICE PASTE

1 onion, roughly chopped

1 red chilli, deseeded

4 garlic cloves

4 teaspoons dried thyme

2 teaspoons ground allspice

1 teaspoon ground cinnamon

½ teaspoon grated nutmeg

2 tablespoons olive oil

1 teaspoon salt

1 teaspoon pepper

CHIVE YOGURT

2 tablespoons chopped chives

300 g (10 oz) natural yogurt

salt and pepper

Spicy sweet potato wedges with sharp, creamy yogurt are great for a veggie barbecue. Jerk paste is easy to make, but use ready-made to save time if you prefer.

1 To make the jerk paste, put all the ingredients into a liquidizer or food processor and whiz to a paste.

2 Cut the sweet potatoes into wedges about 5 mm (¼ inch) thick – thin enough to cook through without burning. Spread the cut surfaces of the wedges with the jerk paste and place under a preheated hot grill or on a barbecue grid. Cook for 5 minutes on each side, or until the sweet potato is tender to the point of a knife and the jerk paste is crunchy and slightly charred.

3 Stir the chives into the yogurt along with some salt and pepper and put into a small bowl.

4 Serve the sweet potato wedges at once while still they are sizzling hot, accompanied by the chive yogurt, wedges of lime and plenty of soft bread, if liked.

Herby Couscous with Red Chilli

SERVES 4

500 ml (17 fl oz)
  vegetable stock

250 g (8 oz) couscous

1 tablespoon olive oil

1 lime

1 lemon

1 mild red chilli,
  deseeded and
  chopped

6 tablespoons chopped
  coriander

4 spring onions, finely
  chopped

salt and pepper

A fast and refreshing accompaniment for dishes such as Lemon-glazed and Seared Haloumi (see page 40), or even on its own, with some salad leaves, for a light meal.

1 Bring the stock to the boil, then add the couscous and olive oil. Cover and set aside, off the heat, for 10–15 minutes.

2 Grate the rind from the lime and lemon, and squeeze the juice out of each; keep the juices separate from each other.

3 Fork through the couscous, then gently stir in the grated citrus rinds, chilli, coriander, spring onion and enough of the squeezed lime and lemon juices to sharpen the mixture to taste: about 1 tablespoon of each.

4 Season with salt and pepper and serve.

Puddings and Cakes

Rhubarb Crumble

SERVES 4–6

900 g (1 lb 13 oz) rhubarb, cut into 2.5-cm (1-inch) lengths

butter, for greasing

75 g (3 oz) sugar

CRUMBLE

250 g (8 oz) self-raising 85% wholemeal flour

175 g (6 oz) butter

175 g (6 oz) demerara sugar

Classic, classic, classic – everyone loves a comforting crumble. I couldn't leave it out, could I?

1 Put the rhubarb into a lightly greased, large, shallow ovenproof dish. Mix in the sugar and make sure the fruit is in an even layer.

2 Put the flour into a mixing bowl and rub in the butter with your fingertips until the mixture looks like fine breadcrumbs and there are no lumps of butter.

3 Add the demerara sugar and mix gently. Spoon the crumble topping over the rhubarb to make an even layer that covers all the fruit.

4 Bake in a preheated oven, 200°C (400°F), Gas Mark 6, for 30–40 minutes, until the crumble is crisp and lightly browned and the rhubarb feels tender when pierced with a skewer. Serve hot.

Dreamy Raspberry and Rose Pavlova

SERVES 6

4 egg whites

250 g (8 oz) caster sugar

2 teaspoons cornflour

1 teaspoon red or white wine vinegar

1 teaspoon vanilla extract

300 ml (½ pint) double cream

2 teaspoons triple-distilled rosewater

375 g (12 oz) raspberries

icing sugar and red or pink rose petals, to decorate

This looks stunning – a lovely treat for a summer party. Flavouring the whipped cream with a hint of rosewater adds an extra dimension.

1 Cover a large baking sheet with nonstick baking paper.

2 Put the egg whites in a spotlessly clean, grease-free bowl and whisk until they stand in peaks.

3 Mix the caster sugar and cornflour, then add to the egg whites in 2–3 batches; whisk all the time to achieve a beautiful, glossy, white meringue mixture. Finally, stir in the wine vinegar and vanilla extract.

4 Spoon the meringue mixture on to the baking paper and gently spread it out into a circle 20–23 cm (8–9 inches) in diameter. Place in a preheated oven, 180°C (350°F), Gas Mark 4, turn the heat down to 150°C (300°F), Gas Mark 2, and bake for 1¼ hours, or until the meringue is crisp. Let it cool in the oven if possible.

5 To finish the pavlova, whip the cream until it forms soft peaks, then whisk in the rosewater. Heap this on top of the meringue, cover with the raspberries, dust with icing sugar and scatter with rose petals. Serve the pavlova as soon as possible, though it's still easy to eat even after 24 hours.

Wholemeal Treacle Tart

SERVES 4

375 g (12 oz) packet
  ready-rolled
  shortcrust pastry

or

100 g (3½ oz) wholemeal
  flour

100 g (3½ oz) plain flour

a pinch of salt

100 g (3½ oz) butter,
  diced

2–3 tablespoons ice-cold
  water

TREACLE
FILLING

100 g (3½ oz) fine
  wholemeal
  breadcrumbs

1 teaspoon lemon juice

350 g (11½ oz) golden
  syrup

If you have time to make it, homemade wholemeal pastry is
wonderful, especially when made with spelt flour. It balances
the sweetness of the golden syrup beautifully.

1 To make your own pastry, whiz the flours, salt and
butter in a food processor until the mixture looks like
breadcrumbs, or rub the butter in by hand. Add enough
water to form a dough. Chill for 30 minutes if possible.

2 Roll out the pastry and use it to line a 20-cm (8-inch)
flan tin. Trim the edges.

3 Put the breadcrumbs into the pastry case to make an
even layer, without pressing them down. Sprinkle with
the lemon juice.

4 Pour the golden syrup on top of the crumbs (you can
do this straight from the jar or tin) so that they are all
evenly covered. Don't try to mix; the crumbs will soak
up the syrup as the tart cooks.

5 Roll out the pastry trimmings and cut them into strips.
Arrange these in a lattice pattern on top of the tart.

6 Bake in a preheated oven, 190°C (375°F), Gas Mark 5,
for 25 minutes, until the pastry is crisp and lightly
browned. Serve warm.

Chocolate Pecan Brownies

MAKES 9

300 g (10 oz) plain chocolate, not too bitter, at least 50% cocoa solids

125 g (4 oz) butter or margarine

4 eggs

2 teaspoons vanilla extract

50 g (2 oz) Barbados sugar

½ teaspoon baking powder

125 g (4 oz) pecan nuts, roughly chopped

These brownies do not contain any flour. They have a crisp, light crust on top and a gooey chocolate centre. Everyone loves them.

1 Line a 20-cm (8-inch) square baking tin with greased greaseproof or nonstick paper.

2 Break the chocolate into pieces and put it into a saucepan with the butter or margarine, and melt gently.

3 Put the eggs into a bowl with the vanilla extract and sugar and whisk at high speed in a food processor or with an electric hand-whisk for about 5 minutes, until the mixture is very thick and pale. Whisk in the melted chocolate and stir in the baking powder and pecan nuts.

4 Pour the mixture into the tin, easing it gently into the corners. Bake in a preheated oven, 180°C (350°F), Gas Mark 4, for 25–30 minutes, or until firm an crisp on top but still squidgy inside. Leave to cool in the tin, then cut into squares.

Vanilla-poached Pears

SERVES 4

175 g (6 oz) caster sugar

rind of ½ lemon, pared
in 1 long strip

1 vanilla pod, split
lengthways

300 ml (½ pint) water

4 pears, peeled, with
stalks intact

HOT CHOCOLATE
SAUCE

100 g (3½ oz) plain
chocolate, broken into
pieces

150 ml (¼ pint) single
or non-dairy cream

VANILLA ICE
CREAM

600 ml (1 pint) double
or whipping cream

400 g (13 oz) can
skimmed condensed
milk

1 teaspoon vanilla
extract

A classic combination that's easy to make and pure decadence to eat!

1 First make the vanilla ice cream. Whip the cream, by hand or with an electric whisk for speed and ease, until soft peaks form. Add the condensed milk and vanilla extract, and whip again until combined. Tip into a suitable container such as a rigid plastic box and freeze until firm.

2 Pour the caster sugar into a saucepan large enough for the pears, and add the lemon rind, vanilla pod and water. Dissolve the sugar over a moderate heat.

3 Put the pears into the liquid, bring the mixture to a gentle simmer, then reduce the heat, cover, and cook for 20–30 minutes, until the pears are tender right through when pierced with a sharp knife or skewer. Remove the pears from the pan using a slotted spoon and place in a serving dish.

4 Turn up the heat and let the liquid boil for about 5 minutes, until it has reduced a little to make a syrup. Discard the lemon rind and pour the syrup, together with the vanilla pod, over the pears. Leave to cool, then refrigerate before serving.

5 To make the chocolate sauce, put the chocolate and cream into a small saucepan and heat gently until the chocolate has melted. Stir well.

6 Serve the pears with the hot chocolate sauce and the vanilla ice cream.

Lemon and Almond Drizzle Cake

SERVES 4

175 g (6 oz) butter, softened

175 g (6 oz) caster sugar

2 eggs

finely grated rind of 1 lemon

175 g (6 oz) self-raising flour

50 g (2 oz) ground almonds

1½ teaspoons baking powder

crème fraîche, to serve

DRIZZLE TOPPING

4 tablespoons lemon juice

150 g (5 oz) icing sugar

BERRIES

500 g (1 lb) mixed berries, such as raspberries, strawberries, blueberries or redcurrants, any stems and hulls removed

caster sugar, to taste

This is a favourite cake in my family, perfect for a birthday, or a treat at any time, and very easy to make.

1 Line a 900 g (1 lb 13 oz) loaf tin with a strip of nonstick baking paper to cover the base and narrow sides.

2 This cake is made by the 'all in one' method: simply put the butter, caster sugar, eggs, lemon rind, flour, ground almonds and baking powder into a bowl and beat by hand or with an electric beater for 2–3 minutes until combined and light.

3 Spoon the mixture into the prepared loaf tin and gently level the top. Bake in a preheated oven, 160°C (325°F), Gas Mark 3, for 40–45 minutes, until it has risen and is firm to a light touch, and a skewer inserted into the centre comes out clean.

4 Five minutes before the cake is done, make the drizzle topping. Mix the lemon juice and icing sugar in a small saucepan, then stir over a gentle heat until the icing sugar has dissolved.

5 As soon as the cake comes out of the oven, prick the top all over and pour the icing sugar mixture over the top. Set aside to cool, then remove the cake from the tin and strip off the paper.

6 Prepare the berries about an hour before you want to eat. Put them into a bowl, sprinkle with caster sugar to taste and set aside for 1 hour, stirring from time to time. Taste and add a little more sugar if necessary.

7 Serve the berries and cake with a bowl of crème fraîche.

Crêpes Suzette

SERVES 4–6

**125 g (4 oz) plain flour –
I use all wholemeal
or half wholemeal,
half white**

a pinch of salt

**2 tablespoons vegetable
oil, plus extra for
brushing**

2 eggs

200 ml (7 fl oz) milk

ORANGE SAUCE

125 g (4 oz) butter

150 g (5 oz) caster sugar

**grated rind and juice
of 3 small to medium
oranges**

**grated rind and juice
of 1 lemon**

**2 tablespoons orange
liqueur, such as
curaçao (optional)**

4 tablespoons brandy

*I enjoy a dish with a bit of drama, and everyone loves this. Make it
ahead of time, then heat it through and flambé it just before serving.*

1 First make the pancakes. Sift the flour and salt into a
bowl, make a well in the middle, add the oil and eggs and
gradually beat in the milk; mix well. Allow to stand for
30 minutes, then beat again before use; alternatively,
process the ingredients in a liquidizer or food processor.

2 Set a frying pan over a moderate heat and brush the base
with vegetable oil. Pour in a little batter, tilting and turning
the pan so that the batter runs all over the base and coats
it thinly. After 20–30 seconds, when the underside of the
pancake is golden brown and the top is just set, turn and
cook on the other side for a few seconds. Transfer to a
plate. Repeat until all the batter is used and you have
about 14 thin pancakes. Cover and keep in a cool place
until needed.

3 To make the orange sauce, put the butter, sugar, grated
rinds and juices, and orange liqueur, if using, into a large
frying pan that you can take to the table, and heat gently
to melt the butter and sugar. Dip a pancake in the sauce,
coating both sides, and fold it in half and in half again, to
make a triangle, then push it to the side of the frying pan.
Repeat with the remaining pancakes and leave them in the
frying pan until you're almost ready to serve them.

4 Just before serving, put the frying pan over a gentle heat
to warm through the sauce and pancakes. When they're
ready, turn the heat up to high for 1 minute, then quickly
pour in the brandy and set it alight. You can take the crêpes
to the table at this point. The flames will die out in a few
seconds, when all the fat has been burnt. Serve immediately.

Fig Tarte Tatin with Ginger Cream

SERVES 4

325 g (11 oz) frozen
   ready-rolled all-butter
   puff pastry, thawed

flour, for dusting

40 g (1½ oz) butter

900 g (1 lb 13 oz) figs,
   halved

40 g (1½ oz) caster sugar

25 g (1 oz) toasted
   flaked almonds, to
   decorate (optional)

GINGER CREAM

275 ml (9 fl oz) double
   cream

3 pieces of preserved
   stem ginger, very
   finely chopped

A tarte Tatin is easy to make, and the combination of the glossy, purple-red figs and crisp, buttery pastry with the ginger-spiked cream is delectable.

1 Roll out the pastry on a lightly floured surface to make it a bit thinner if you can, then cut a circle 1 cm (½ inch) larger than the top of a 20-cm (8-inch) tarte Tatin pan or cake tin.

2 Melt the butter in the tarte Tatin pan or in a frying pan. Add the figs, cut-sides down, and the caster sugar. Cook over a high heat for about 6 minutes, until the figs are slightly browned and caramelized. If you're baking the tart in a cake tin, put the figs into it, cut-sides down, and scrape in all the gooey juice from the frying pan.

3 Put the pastry on top, tucking it down around the figs at the sides. Prick the pastry, then bake in a preheated oven, 200°C (400°F), Gas Mark 6, for 20–25 minutes, until crisp and golden brown.

4 Meanwhile, make the ginger cream. Whip the cream until it is standing in soft peaks, then fold in the ginger. Transfer to a bowl and chill until required.

5 To serve, loosen the tart with a knife, then invert it over a plate. The figs will be on top. Scatter with toasted flaked almonds, if using, and leave the tart to settle for a couple of minutes before serving it with the ginger cream.

Magical Instant Cheesecake

SERVES 6

- 200 g (7 oz) digestive biscuits
- 25 g (1 oz) butter
- 100 g (3½ oz) plain chocolate, broken into pieces
- 300 g (10 oz) smooth medium- or low-fat cream cheese
- 50 g (2 oz) caster sugar
- 150 ml (¼ pint) double cream (normal, not 'extra thick')
- 1 tablespoon lemon juice
- 250 g (8 oz) raspberries
- 6 heaped tablespoons seedless raspberry jam

This is a wonderful, instant cheesecake that's delectable eaten as soon as it's made. You can also make it in advance, but leave the glazing until the last minute.

1 Put the digestive biscuits into a plastic bag, close the top and crush to a powder with a rolling pin.

2 Put the butter and chocolate into a saucepan and melt over a gentle heat, stirring often to prevent sticking.

3 Mix the crushed biscuits with the melted chocolate mixture and press firmly into the base of a 20-cm (8-inch) springform cake tin or flan tin. Set aside, in the fridge if possible, while you make the topping.

4 Mix the cream cheese with the caster sugar and pour in the cream. Beat with a fork or whisk until the mixture is thick. Add the lemon juice and stir gently: the mixture will become even thicker.

5 Spread the cream cheese mixture evenly over the crumb base, then arrange the raspberries on top.

6 Melt the raspberry jam over a gentle heat, then spoon it over the raspberries to make a sweet, shiny glaze.

7 Serve at once, or keep the cheesecake in a cool place for an hour or so. If it needs to wait any longer than this, leave off the glaze and add it later, so that it is at its bright and shiny best when served.

Whiskey Cream Banoffi

SERVES 4–6

250 g (8 oz) digestive biscuits

125 g (4 oz) butter, melted

2–3 large bananas

400 g (13 oz) can caramelized condensed milk

300 ml (½ pint) double cream

4 tablespoons Bailey's cream liqueur

25 g (1 oz) dark chocolate, grated

Everyone loves this! Leave out the Bailey's, though, if you're serving it to children; it will still be gorgeous.

1 Put the biscuits in a large polythene bag, close the top and crush with a rolling pin to make fine crumbs. Mix the biscuit crumbs with the melted butter, then press into the base of a 20–23-cm (8–9-inch) flan dish. If there's time, put this into the fridge for 10–15 minutes to chill.

2 Peel the bananas and slice each in half lengthways. Lay the slices of banana, cut-sides down, in the flan dish, cutting them as necessary to make them fit.

3 Spoon the caramelized condensed milk evenly over the bananas, to cover them.

4 Whip the cream with the Bailey's until it stands in soft peaks, then spoon it over the caramelized condensed milk, taking it to the edges of the dish. Sprinkle the grated chocolate over the top. Chill until required – if anything, this tastes even better after 24 hours.

Sangria Fruit Salad

SERVES 4

juice and finely grated
   rind of 1 orange

4 tablespoons caster
   sugar

4 tablespoons Spanish
   red wine

1 tablespoon brandy

1 tablespoon Cointreau

2 oranges, skin and pith
   removed, cut into
   segments

1 apple, peeled and
   sliced

2 peaches, thinly sliced,
   stones removed

175 g (6 oz) white
   grapes, halved and
   deseeded

mint sprigs

ALMOND
SHORTBREADS

175 g (6 oz) butter

50 g (2 oz) caster sugar

175 g (6 oz) plain white
   flour

50 g (2 oz) ground
   almonds

icing sugar, for dusting

A fruit salad with sunshine flavours and tender, melt-in-the-mouth shortbread to go with it.

1 Put the orange juice and rind into a large bowl with the caster sugar, red wine, brandy and Cointreau. Add all the prepared fruit and some of the mint sprigs and stir gently. Set aside for at least 30 minutes in a cool place until needed.

2 To make the almond shortbreads, beat together the butter and caster sugar until light and fluffy, then stir in the flour and ground almonds to make a soft dough. Form the dough into 16 even-sized ovals and place well apart on baking sheets lined with nonstick baking paper. Press the ovals lightly with the prongs of a fork.

3 Bake in a preheated oven, 160°C (325°F), Gas Mark 3, for 15 minutes, or until set and lightly coloured. Cool on the baking sheets, then dredge with icing sugar. Serve with the fruit salad, decorated with the remaining mint sprigs.

Mixed Melon Compote

SERVES 8

1 small Charantais melon

1 small Galia melon

1 mini watermelon

caster sugar or light clear honey

8 tablespoons crème de menthe, or to taste

mint leaves, to decorate

This makes enough for a party – for 4 people, use half a Charantais and half a Galia melon, and about one-third of a mini watermelon, and reduce other ingredients proportionately.

1 Remove the rinds and seeds from the melons and cut the flesh into chunks.

2 Put the melon chunks into a large bowl and sweeten as necessary with caster sugar or honey, then stir in the crème de menthe to taste.

3 Serve in individual bowls, decorated with mint leaves.

Pink Champagne Granita

SERVES 4
200 ml (7 fl oz) water
225 g (7½ oz) caster
   sugar, plus
   2 tablespoons
1 bottle pink
   Champagne
375 g (12 oz) raspberries

Nothing says 'celebration' like this Pink Champagne Granita, and it's very easy to make.

1 Put the water into a saucepan with the 225 g (7½ oz) caster sugar. Heat gently until the sugar has dissolved, then bring to the boil and remove the syrup from the heat. Leave to cool.

2 Mix the cooled sugar syrup with the Champagne. Pour into a shallow container so that the liquid is about 1 cm (½ inch) deep and freeze, stirring from time to time as the syrup starts to freeze around the edges. Because of the alcohol in the Champagne, the granita will take up to 4 hours to freeze, and will never become rock hard, so it can be used straight from the freezer. It's fine to make it the day before needed.

3 To serve, first toss the raspberries in the 2 tablespoons caster sugar and set aside for a few minutes until the sugar has dissolved. Put a few raspberries into each of 4 serving glasses. Give the granita a quick stir with a fork, then scrape some into the glasses, on top of the raspberries. Continue to layer the raspberries and granita in the glasses, then serve immediately.

Affogato with Almond Tuiles

SERVES 4

600 ml (1 pint) double
  or whipping cream

400 g (13 oz) can
  skimmed condensed
  milk

150 ml (¼ pint) hot,
  strong espresso
  coffee, to serve

ALMOND TUILES

1 egg white

50 g (2 oz) caster sugar

25 g (1 oz) plain flour,
  sifted

25 g (1 oz) butter, melted

40 g (1½ oz) flaked
  almonds

flavourless vegetable
  oil, such as grapeseed,
  for greasing

*This simple ice cream is the easiest and best I know. It's perfect
served like this, with hot, strong espresso poured over it and a crisp
almond biscuit.*

1 First make the affogato. Whip the cream, with an electric
whisk for speed and ease, or by hand, until soft peaks form.
Add the condensed milk to the cream and whip until
combined. Tip into a suitable container – a rigid plastic
box is ideal – and freeze until firm.

2 To make the tuiles, whisk the egg white until stiff,
then whisk in the caster sugar. Add the flour and butter
alternately to make a smooth mixture. Place big teaspoons
of the mixture well apart on a baking sheet lined with
nonstick baking paper (you'll probably get about 4 to
a large sheet) and, using the back of the spoon, spread
the mixture out to make rounds about 10 cm (4 inches)
in diameter. Sprinkle the top of each with the flaked
almonds, then bake for 4–5 minutes in a preheated oven,
180°C (350°F), Gas Mark 4, until the tuiles are set and
lightly browned, especially around the edges.

3 Remove the tuiles from the oven and set aside for
1–2 minutes, until they are firm enough to be lifted from
the baking sheet. Meanwhile, oil a rolling pin. Drape the
tuiles over the rolling pin so that they become curved as
they cool. Once they're cool, remove them to a wire rack.

4 Continue with the remaining mixture to make about
16 tuiles. When all of them are cold, store them in an
airtight tin until needed.

5 To serve, scoop the affogato into 4 bowls. Pour about
2 tablespoons of the hot espresso over each and serve
immediately, with the almond tuiles.

Index